MELTDOWN

Inside the Soviet Economy

MELTDOWN
Inside the Soviet Economy

**Paul Craig Roberts
and Karen LaFollette**
Institute for Political Economy

CATO
INSTITUTE
Washington D.C.

Library of Congress Cataloging-in-Publication Data

Roberts, Paul Craig, 1939–
  Meltdown : inside the Soviet economy / Paul Craig Roberts and Karen
LaFollette.
      p. cm.
    Includes bibliographical references and index.
    ISBN 0-932790-79-8 : $19.95.   ISBN 0-932790-80-1 (pbk.) : $9.95
    1. Soviet Union—Economic conditions—1985–   2. Soviet Union—
  Economic policy—1986–   3. Central planning—Soviet Union.
  4. Communism—Soviet Union. I. LaFollette, Karen, 1960–   .
  II. Title.
  HC336.26.R63   1990   90–2519
  330.947'0854—dc20   CIP

Printed in the United States of America.

                        CATO INSTITUTE
                   224 Second Street, S.E.
                   Washington, D.C. 20003

Contents

Dedication

For Becky Ellen, Stephanie, and Pendaran, and for Tony, Judy, and Brian.

Preface

The explanations that people in the West have been given about the performance and success of Soviet communism have left them unprepared for its dramatic failure—indeed, so much so that our account, which relies heavily on Soviet sources, raises problems of believability. How can an economy that can put men in space and confront the United States with equal, if not superior, military capability be consistent with the living standards portrayed in this book?

Inevitably, some critics will attack our use of Soviet sources by saying that people who are suddenly free to speak their own minds will exaggerate while letting off the steam they have accumulated over decades. There may be some truth in this skeptical view of the new Soviet press. Nevertheless, Soviet officials themselves take the letters and accounts in their press seriously, and they speak openly of the dire economic and political challenge that they face. If the Soviet Union is not confronted with failure, then we are witnessing the gratuitous self-destruction of the power and perks of a powerful political class—the Communist Party. Such an event would surely demand that scholars abandon their materialistic explanations of society and history.

A Western public that places its hopes for world peace on Soviet leader Mikhail Gorbachev and his policies of *glasnost*, or openness, and *perestroika*, or restructuring of the economy, should be apprised of the depth of economic, political, and social crisis in the Soviet Union. We believe that this book will leave the reader with a sober view of Soviet reality as well as with a basis for hope.

Acknowledgments

We are pleased that the Cato Institute is publishing the Institute for Political Economy's first book. We are very grateful to Edward H. Crane and David Boaz for their interest and editorial help. We very much admire the integrity of Cato's voice and are pleased to be part of their program.

We are grateful to the Institute for Political Economy's donors and trustees who have supported this project. The Institute for Political Economy is fortunate in having a diverse group of supporters with different interests who fund independent research.

In particular, we would like to thank George Champion for his leadership of our Board of Trustees, Bill Simon for his leadership of our Advisory Board, and Sir James Goldsmith and Ambassador Evan Galbraith for leading our Political Economy Council. The generosity of Jack Stephens, Roger Milliken, Robert Krieble, the Olin Foundation, the Earhart Foundation, the ADM Foundation, the J.M. Foundation, the Grace Foundation, and other donors, whose support we are privileged to have, made this book possible.

The staff of the Soviet and East European Studies Program at the Center for Strategic and International Studies cheerfully helped us with various details of Soviet information.

1. Introduction

On February 17, 1988, Soviet leader Mikhail Gorbachev jolted the entire world when he told the Central Committee of the Communist Party that, except for vodka sales and the higher prices paid for Soviet oil, the Soviet economy had not grown for 20 years.[1] The Central Intelligence Agency and Soviet specialists at Western universities were still reeling when top Soviet economist Abel Aganbegyan landed another punch:

> In the period 1981–85 there was practically no economic growth. Unprecedented stagnation and crisis occurred, during the period 1979–82, when production of 40% of all industrial goods actually fell. Agriculture declined (throughout this period it failed to reach the 1978 output levels). The use of productive resources sharply declined and the rate of growth of all indicators of efficiency in social production slowed down, in effect the productivity of labour did not increase.[2]

In April 1988, after Gorbachev's speech and its dissemination in the West, the CIA and the Defense Intelligence Agency still put a positive gloss on the Soviet economy, telling the Joint Economic Committee of Congress that the Soviet economy grew roughly 2 percent yearly during 1981–85. In their report to the JEC, our intelligence agencies painted a picture of unbroken progress for the Soviet economy, which, they said, grew at a rate of 2.2 percent yearly from 1976 to 1980, 3.1 percent from 1971 to 1975, and 5

---

[1]Communique on the Plenary Session of the Central Committee of the Communist Party of the Soviet Union, *Pravda* and *Izvestiya*, February 18, 1988, p. 1. Also, Daniel Franklin, "The Soviet Economy," in *The Economist*, April 9, 1988, and Abram Bergson, Radio Free Europe, Radio Liberty, "Gorbachev on Soviet Growth Rate," March 25, 1988.

[2]Abel Aganbegyan, *The Economic Challenge of Perestroika* (Bloomington and Indianapolis: Indiana University Press, 1988), p. 3.

1

percent from 1966 to 1970.[3] These estimates were reductions from the previous, more optimistic line.

The CIA has not been unique in exaggerating Soviet economic achievement. Since the Bolshevik Revolution, Western analysts have had a history of overestimating the accomplishments of the Soviet economy. Government and academic specialists alike predicted great success for the system of central planning that was first implemented by Lenin, finding a potency in the Soviet planned economy that would surpass our "chaotic" market economy. Perhaps the high-water mark in glorifying "Soviet-type planning" was a 1979 World Bank report, "Romania: The Industrialization of an Agrarian Economy under Socialist Planning." According to this report, "comprehensive economic planning, which was made possible by the state's control of the major productive resources and its monopoly over foreign trade," produced an average annual growth rate of 9.8 percent between 1950 and 1975, outstripping even the success of Japan and Hong Kong. As the *Wall Street Journal* noted in an August 10, 1979, editorial, using these lofty growth rates to project backward the World Bank's estimate of Romanian per capita income produced a figure too low to sustain life. "We have heard exaggerated claims made for central economic planning," the *Journal* wrote, "but never that it resurrected a whole nation from the dead."

Many Westerners were seduced by the Soviets' talk of systematically planning and controlling a national economy. Some progressive intellectuals had lost faith in capitalism and found central planning emotionally satisfying and exciting. Many scientists accepted the Marxists' claims that communism was based on science; in Great Britain there was an active movement among scientists calling on government to plan science in the interests of society.

Since capitalism was regarded as a system that elevated greed above social needs, the Great Depression in the 1930s shook what confidence intellectuals had left in the market. Laissez faire was officially pronounced dead, first by President Herbert Hoover's

---

[3]"Gorbachev's Economic Program: Problems Emerge," Central Intelligence Agency report presented to Subcommittee on National Security Economics of the Joint Economic Committee of Congress on April 13, 1988, p. 61.

extra-market measures,[4] and then by President Franklin D. Roosevelt's New Deal. Rexford Tugwell, assistant secretary of the Treasury under Roosevelt, and Howard Hill observed in their 1934 book that

> the challenge of Russia to America does not lie in the merits of the Soviet system, although they may prove to be considerable. The challenge lies rather in the idea of planning, of purposeful, intelligent control over economic affairs. This, it seems, we must accept as a guide to our economic life to replace the decadent notions of a laissez-faire philosophy.[5]

Julian Huxley, noted British scientist, concurred: "Proper planning is itself the application of scientific method to human affairs."[6] In praising the efforts of the Soviets, Huxley remarked,

> But while the Five Year Plan is without doubt of the greatest importance, it is in a sense only an incident, only a symptom. It is an incident in a long series of plans; it is a symptom of a new spirit, the spirit of science introduced into politics and industry.[7]

Thus, from the start the hopes inspired by planning led to an overstatement of the case. Forgetting completely the American experience, one traveler through the Soviet Union explained,

> Economically, Russia calls for a collectivist society. Its fields are vast, its horizons remote: only a people organized *as a whole* can dominate the physical vagueness of Russia. It is the lack of such a dominance that left Russia impotent for a thousand years.[8]

[4]Charles A. Beard and William Beard, *The American Leviathan: The Republic in the Machine Age* (New York: The Macmillan Co., 1930), pp. 643–44. "While insisting that government and business should be considered separate entities, the President [Hoover] proceeded on the theory of planned national economy rather than on the assumption of fatalistic helplessness common to classical economic doctrines."

[5]Rexford Guy Tugwell and Howard C. Hill, *Our Economic Society and Its Problems: A Study of American Levels of Living and How to Improve Them* (New York: Harcourt, Brace and Co., 1934), p. 527.

[6]Julian Huxley, *A Scientist Among the Soviets* (New York: Harper & Brothers, 1932), p. 61.

[7]Huxley, p. 60.

[8]Waldo Frank, *Dawn in Russia: The Record of a Journey* (New York: Charles Scribner's Sons, 1932), p. 240.

Tugwell and Hill agreed, explaining that "there is little evidence that production in Russia is less than it would be under capitalism."[9]

In 1957 Stanford University professor Paul Baran, in his influential book *The Political Economy of Growth*, explained away the heinous crimes and devastation wrought by the Soviet regime in its efforts to create the new economic system:

> For a considerable time both irrationality and error will mar also the socialist order. Crimes will be committed, abuses will be perpetrated, cruelty and injustice will be inevitable. Nor can it be expected that no mistakes will be made in the management of its affairs. Plans will be wrongly drawn up, resources will be wasted, bridges will be built where none are needed, factories constructed where more wheat should have been planted.[10]

Baran concluded that these mistakes were minor stuff compared to the victory of banishing the irrationality of the market from economic life:

> What is decisive, however, is that irrationality will henceforth not be—as it is under capitalism—*inherent* in the structure of society. It will not be the unavoidable outgrowth of a social system based on exploitation, national prejudice, and incessantly cultivated superstition. It will become a residue of a historical past, deprived of its socioeconomic foundation, rendered rootless by the disappearance of classes, by the end of exploitation of men by men.[11]

Baran wholeheartedly sympathized with Stalin:

> The attainment of a social order in which economic and cultural growth will be possible on the basis of ever-increasing rational domination by man of the inexhaustible forces of nature is a task exceeding in scope and challenge everything thus far accomplished in the course of history.[12]

Western observers continued to admire the wonders of central planning throughout the decades marked by government-imposed

[9]Tugwell and Hill, pp. 521–22.

[10]Paul Baran, *The Political Economy of Growth* (New York: Monthly Review Press, 1962), p. 299. First published in 1957.

[11]Baran, p. 299.

[12]Ibid., p. 297.

famines, purges, and slave labor camps. In 1932, while the terrible famine raged in the Ukraine, killing 7 million, Huxley enthused:

> The first result of the plan, then, will be for Russia to reach a high level in heavy industry, even though this means keeping the food and comforts of the people at a low level. The next step will be to raise light industry to a corresponding level. . . . If all goes well, this stage, when both industry and standard of living rival those of advanced capitalist countries, will be reached in fifteen or twenty years.[13]

Fifty-eight years later, the Soviets are further behind than ever. Indeed, even people in Third World countries such as Brazil, Malaysia, and the Ivory Coast have easier access to goods and enjoy higher standards of living than Soviet citizens.

Thanks to Mikhail Gorbachev and Soviet economists such as Abel Aganbegyan and Leonid Abalkin, almost everyone today understands that central planning does not work. Still, the Soviet economy remains a mystery to Westerners, and the Soviet consumer's deprivation is unimaginable to those accustomed to a convenient economic life filled with a rich variety of foodstuffs and consumer goods.

In this book we describe the irrational life of Soviet producers, the monstrous deprivation of Soviet consumers, and the ideological origins of the Soviet economy that have resulted in a system unable to bear the weight of being a superpower. We spell out the challenges that Gorbachev and his successors face. The penultimate chapter deals with the privatization of the Soviet economy. In the last chapter we document the failure of Western experts and pundits to create a true picture of the Soviet system.

For its own sake, the West must do a better job of understanding Soviet experience, both past and present.

---

[13]Huxley, p. 98.

2. The Soviet Producer

Picture the life of factory directors in the Soviet Union. They escape the stressful, competitive pressures of having to make a profit, please finicky consumers, acquire financing, and devise advertising and marketing strategies—all of which make or break companies in the West. Factory directors do not agonize over what to produce, nor do they do expensive market research to figure out what consumers want. Their factory quotas, or plans, tell them what to produce. All they need to do is meet their plans. The state is waiting for their production; it will take everything the factories produce. For instance, a director manufactures 10,000 pairs of shoes and delivers them to the state. That director is not touched by Western problems and is free to devote all his energies to production.

Furthermore, officially factory directors do not even have to go out and find supplies for the manufacture of their products. The state does it for them. Their worst headache could be labor-management relations—but even that is not too bad, because the workers cannot go on strike anyway.

On paper the Soviet manager has a wonderful, cushy life, but in reality, nothing could be further from the truth. American managers have it easy compared to their Soviet counterparts. Soviet managers cannot rely on the state to set a reasonable plan for their factories, nor can they rely on it to provide them with the inputs they need to meet that plan. The official system obstructs their every effort to increase efficiency, get supplies, and introduce innovative changes at the factory. To top it all off, the Soviet manager is a hostage to politics to a degree unthinkable to the American manager.

This chapter describes the world of the Soviet producer. To begin with, the measures of success for Soviet managers are quite different from those of their Western counterparts. Success does not depend on satisfying the users of their products or on making a profit. The Soviet system is geared toward satisfying the planners' needs and wants; consumers' wishes are not a consideration. Soviet managers work to please the state agency with jurisdiction over their firms. Each manager's superior is satisfied if the firm fulfills or overfulfills the plan for the year.

Gross Output Indicator

The plan is all important, and the leadership extols it as law. The targets of the plan are expressed in terms of "gross output"—goods measured by volume, surface area, weight, or number. The factory concentrates all production efforts on meeting gross output targets. This type of target leads directly to the production of poor quality, substandard, and useless goods.

If the factory's output is specified by weight, its products will be heavy. If the plan is expressed in volume, the goods produced will be very thin or flimsy. Examples of unforeseen outcomes are everywhere: Khrushchev himself cited chandeliers that were so heavy they pulled down ceilings; the Soviet press reported roofing metal so thick it collapsed the building it was supposed to cover. The press also cited paper-thin roofing metal that blows off the building with the first gust of wind and structural boards that are either too heavy (endangering the floor below them) or too light (collapsing the roof above them).[1]

Periodically, the ministries have tried to correct problems such as production of overly heavy nails. They changed a firm's indicator to number instead of weight, for instance. But this only caused the output assortment to be skewed to small sizes. Switching back and forth between gross output measures merely causes different distortions to appear.

The Soviet leadership has made repeated attempts to modify the gross output indicator to try to foster usable production. The "net output" indicator was introduced in 1957 to try to overcome the distortions of the gross output indicator. Under net output, the targets were denominated in terms of volume, weight, or number but included a measure of value added to the product. However, exhorting the factories to further processing still did not produce adequate goods for the consumer.

[1]The problem of collapsing roofs and structural walls is such a frequent occurrence that it is mentioned even in articles on unrelated topics. We found seven citations in *Pravda* alone over a two-year period.

During the modest Kosygin reforms of 1965, the gross output indicator was modified to emphasize the value of goods (as determined by the arbitrary fixed prices) and was called the "realized output" target. Producers responded by using materials with the most favorable prices in their production processes, regardless of whether the resources were appropriate for use in producing the items. This indicator also caused firms to produce whatever assortment of goods that maximized their profit under the rules, regardless of demand. For example, 40,000 handkerchiefs would be produced instead of an assortment of linens that a factory was directed to manufacture, because the profit per handkerchief for the factory was higher than that of other items in the factory plan.

The consumer did not benefit from these reforms. Emphasis on one aspect of production merely led to the neglect of others. In reality, the gross output indicator still reigns supreme in the Soviet Union, by whatever name it is called.

Since the supervising ministry or agency is rarely the final user of the firm's products and is most concerned with how the production looks on paper, the firm has leeway to sacrifice quality and to manipulate production statistics in order to improve its performance on paper.

In fulfilling the enterprise plan, the director cannot simply concentrate on straightforward production to meet the agreed-upon targets of his gross output plan. His job is immeasurably complicated by an avalanche of contradictory directives and laws raining down from above, which often insist on arbitrary changes in the plan.

Instead of tying him to a set course, however, the confusion provides the director with a measure of flexibility as he sets about fulfilling the plan. He manipulates the situation to his own financial advantage by selecting the directives and plan components that will enable him to maximize his bonus and, in the process, that of his staff and personnel. He ignores less-favorable instructions. Because workers' salaries are abysmally low, following the manager in his chosen course is in the workers' strong interest.

Incentives to fulfill and overfulfill the factory plan commonly take the form of monetary premiums and bonuses awarded to employees by the supervising ministry. Fulfillment of each component of the plan carries with it a corresponding monetary reward.

Profit in the Western sense has no meaning for the Soviet manager. If by chance the firm does turn a profit, it is simply taxed away by the state. The director's interest in profit is limited to the premiums tied to the subsidiary and essentially meaningless profit component of the plan.

The Perversity of Production

The incentive structure inherent to the gross output system leads to perverse production outcomes. Examples of its effects are everywhere.

In the petroleum industry, for instance, geologists assigned to drill for oil are rewarded with premiums if they drill a specified number of meters per month. The geologists quite logically react by drilling only shallow holes, since the deeper they go, the slower the progress of the drilling. As a result, some geological expeditions in the Republic of Kazakhstan have not discovered a valuable deposit for many years, but they are considered successful because they have fulfilled their quota in terms of meters drilled. The geologists and ministers are paid handsomely for their efforts, everyone goes out and gets drunk, and no one cares that the whole exercise has been an extraordinary waste of time and money. Groups that do conscientiously turn up deposits are often financial losers under the perverse incentives.[2]

Examples of the perverse incentive structure dot the Soviet landscape in the form of numerous unfinished buildings. Financially, construction managers find it beneficial to begin new building projects before they finish ones already under way, because they receive premiums according to the number of square meters under construction. (It is also far easier to get the ministry's approval to begin a new building than to get funds to continue an ongoing project.) Hence, Marshall Goldman reported in 1980 that the Law School at Moscow State University had been under construction for more than a decade,[3] and *Pravda* reported in 1986 that the Turist Hotel had been under construction for about the same time.[4] Unfinished

---

[2]Marshall I. Goldman, *USSR in Crisis* (New York: W. W. Norton & Co., 1983), p. 38.

[3]Goldman, p. 40.

[4]"Why a New Site," *Pravda*, July 9, 1986, p. 2.

buildings and factories slowly come to ruin, with thistles taking over abandoned construction sites.

The snail's pace of construction work resulting from the perverse incentives of the Soviet system has far-reaching consequences. Interminably long delays in the finishing of factory buildings throw off plant production dates and wreak havoc on the economy. On the morning of its construction deadline, the assembly building at the Kommunar Factory located in the southern Ukraine seemed finished from a distance, but that happy illusion disappeared with the discovery that although the walls and roof were plainly in evidence, that most essential feature—the floor—was missing. And 56 million rubles worth of expensive imported equipment deteriorated in warehouses because it could not be installed in the specially designed building. This, in turn, hopelessly delayed start-up production of a new model automobile.[5]

Firms are awarded premiums for buildings finished before the prescribed deadline, which leads to all sorts of deceptions, such as declaring buildings finished though they lack roofs and plumbing. Unusable buildings are declared finished every day, and premiums are pocketed for timely performance. Inspections turn up all sorts of problems that somehow escaped the notice of the myriad officials involved: schools without plumbing or lights, hospitals that can accept no patients because of crumbling structural walls, and factories that are supposed to start production with no electricity.[6]

Elaborate dedication ceremonies often hide deception. Great fanfare and celebration met completion of one regional power plant that had been awaited for five years. A 1973 *Trud* report disclosed, however, that the plant was really an empty shell; it had no electricity generator and, therefore, could contribute nothing to the power grid. Still, the state companies and ministries pushed ahead with the plant's dedication, all eyes on the deadline premiums.

The following report shows the extraordinary lengths to which officials went to get an apartment building, which had been robbed of a number of bathtubs, declared finished:

> So how could they hand over the apartment building as completed? They could not confess to the construction

[5]"There's a Roof, but No Floor," letter to *Pravda*, October 3, 1986, p.2.
[6]S. Akbarov, "Wherever You Go," *Pravda*, February 18, 1987, p. 2.

11

superintendent, of course—he was triumphantly showing the official acceptance committee around the first stair landing, yes, and he did not omit to take them into every bathroom too and show them each tub. And then he took the committee to the second-floor landing, and the third, not hurrying there either, and kept going into all the bathrooms—and meanwhile the adroit and experienced [laborers], under the leadership of an experienced foreman plumber, broke bathtubs out of the apartments on the first landing, hauled them upstairs on tiptoe to the fourth floor and hurriedly installed and puttied them in before the committee's arrival.[7]

Even a scientific museum, darling of the Central Committee, could not escape this syndrome. Amid much hoopla, the Memorial Space Museum was opened in 1981 by 20 ministries and government departments. Prizes and bonuses were distributed and lines of museum-goers formed. The museum's director reported,

> But few knew that everyone who entered the underground building risked becoming the victim of an accident, ranging from fire to the simple collapse of structural components that were ready to crush dozens of sightseers.[8]

The situation entirely suited the Moscow cultural administration, however, because the plan for museum tours was being overfulfilled.

The construction industry is a showcase of the perverse incentive structure. *Pravda* correspondent V. Molchanov complains that construction workers create havoc with underground cable networks. They excavate haphazardly with no thought of avoiding the cables. Ruptures occur and the electricity goes off in large parts of the city, but workers are unconcerned. Although they must pay fines of 10 to 25 rubles, they are compensated many times over by bonuses for overfulfillment of the plan for "cubage" of dirt brought to the surface.[9]

[7]Aleksandr I. Solzhenitsyn, *The Gulag Archipelago 1918–1956*, abridged ed. (New York: Harper & Row, 1985), p. 294.

[8]*Pravda*, April 5, 1988.

[9]*Pravda*, July 3, 1987.

12

In the United States we are incensed by corporate corruption, and we unleash moral indignation at crooked officials who are out to make a fast buck. But when we look at the Soviet Union, we see that state companies and ministries daily conspire to defraud the system. It seems that everyone is involved, from the construction worker who intentionally puts up the shoddy wall, to the high-level ministry official who signs the completion certificate and knows full well that the building does not have plumbing or electricity. Obviously, many people are more concerned with getting their premiums and bonuses for good performance than they are about whether something works correctly.

Shoddy housing construction caused widespread death and destruction when an earthquake measuring only 6.9 on the Richter scale occurred in Soviet Armenia. An estimated 20,000 people died from the massive collapse of buildings in the area. Whole villages and towns were destroyed, along with two-thirds of Leninakan (the second largest city) and half of Kirovakan (third largest). According to Gerald Wieczorek of the U.S. Geological Survey, similar earthquakes would cause minimal damage in the United States. In his view, it didn't take much to collapse multistoried buildings made of unreinforced concrete, low-grade masonry, and prefabricated concrete sections haphazardly hooked together.[10]

The perpetual shortage of spare parts and the dismal repair service in every Soviet industry can also be traced to the bizarre incentives of producing to meet gross output targets. One planning engineer in a machinery manufacturing plant explains the lack of spare parts:

> The director of this factory figures that if he puts out 100 machines with the proper quantity of spare parts, he does not get a premium. But if he puts out 102 machines and no spare parts, then the chief engineer and all the technical personnel get premiums. There is not enough stimulus for producing spare parts.[11]

[10]Telephone interview with Gerald Wieczorek, U.S. Geological Survey, December 5, 1988.

[11]Joseph S. Berliner, *Factory and Manager in the USSR* (Cambridge: Harvard University Press, 1957), p. 33.

13

Indeed, factories suffer such a severe shortage of spare parts that workers often "undress" finished goods to acquire the needed parts before delivery.

Repairs are a nightmare. In a typical instance, a state farm in Minsk sent its trucks to be repaired by the Slutsky Auto Repair Shop. The repair shop insisted on full payment before the farmers could inspect the trucks. Little wonder that they wanted their money first, because even poorly fixed trucks would have been an improvement over the truth: not only had the trucks not been fixed at all, but they had been stripped bare of parts they started out with. The farm's driver had to haul them back to the farm where two weeks were spent replacing the parts and fixing the stripped trucks. Too late, the farmers learned that sizeable bribes must be paid to repair people to ensure the intended outcome. Members of the repair shop staff have turned their employer into their own private gold mine.[12]

The Soviet press cites numerous instances of simple repairs that cannot be done because of an acute shortage of a tiny part. One woman was told she could not have her sewing machine fixed because a fastening screw was missing from the machine, a part that for years has been almost impossible to find. The unavailability of parts afflicts items as diverse as washing machines, refrigerators, irons, hair dryers, mixers, calculators, saws, and drills, reducing them to junk without the needed replacement parts.

The Material Supply System

In establishing the system of production according to a plan denominated in gross output targets, the Soviet leadership stripped prices of their relation to market value and established a central supply system that would abolish markets for factors of production.

The Soviet managers suffer from planned prices. Many resources are priced ridiculously cheap and thus are never available. On the other hand, electronic goods and modern machinery are extremely expensive and, partly because of the cost, can rarely be obtained to improve production.

Hand in hand with the pricing system, the centralized supply system steps in to make the managers' lives miserable. Although the system is touted as the cornerstone of economic planning,

[12]"And They Said, Money First," letter to *Pravda*, June 6, 1986, p. 3.

its failures are notorious. It cannot begin to efficiently distribute resources to state firms. Once managers obtain the needed approval for purchasing of supplies—an excruciating process in itself—they find that the supplies are never in stock. Approval to purchase is no better than a "hunting license" for managers to track down materials any way they can through official and unofficial channels.

The economy is plagued by shortages because the system forces an artificial disconnection between the producer and the consumer. Because producers work only to please planners, production output is largely unsuitable for the user's needs. Because every factory is a consumer of inputs produced by other factories, generalized shortages result in the frenetic search for usable materials.

Factory directors in economic sectors that receive low priority suffer most from supply bottlenecks and are compelled to hire supply agents to track down sources of needed supplies. Agents use the official system, personal connections, and illegal trade transactions between other firms to obtain the inputs.

A shadowy character has arisen from the universal shortages: the *tolkach*. Managers across the country cry for the *tolkach's* services. The *tolkachi* are people who have a network of personal connections enabling them to locate a source for virtually any item. They extensively use the black market in stolen state goods and are provided with expense accounts to wine and dine and bribe anyone who can wrangle supplies. Often, tolkachi are freelancers employed by more than one company. They are never officially on any company's payroll but are paid through ingenious juggling of accounts devised by chief accountants. The economy's dependence on the tolkach drives home the failure of central planning.

Other managers travel a different route to overcome input shortages. Some have tooled their factories to manufacture most of the inputs they need in production. This trend toward self-sufficiency has led to gross inefficiencies because the firm ends up producing very little of the product in which it was originally specialized. Consider the Andropov plant that is the only producer of roller presses for offset printing in the Soviet Union.[13] The printing industry throughout the country clamors for roller presses, but only one-third of orders have been fulfilled. Under a normally functioning

---

[13]*Pravda*, February 9, 1988.

market economy, the factory would be scurrying to speed production of its product. The Andropov plant, however, produces fewer and fewer roller presses each year. Production of the presses has fallen to half of the factory's 1968 output. Why? The plant has such trouble getting materials from its suppliers that it must produce everything it needs itself, "right down to the last bolt." In the words of chief engineer Aleksandr Mikhailovich Vaneev, "We make many tens of thousands of different parts; we've turned into a small-batch and one-of-a-kind production outfit," which is hardly suited to the fast production of roller presses.

Endemic shortages and late delivery of materials have led to the widespread practice known as "storming." Yearly plans of enterprises across the country begin and end at the same time, wreaking havoc on production. Firms cannot coordinate their production schedules among themselves, because they are not supposed to deal with each other directly. Production typically functions on a monthly cycle, with three discernible periods that are called hibernation, hot time, and feverish frenzy or storming.

Since supplies rarely arrive until after the 15th of the month, nobody actually works during the first two weeks. Workers goof off, sleep on the job, and disappear for hours or even days at a time. The delivery of supplies around the 15th or the 20th cranks production into a hot time, which rises to a storm at the end of the month as managers strain to meet monthly targets. Workers are forced to put in 12- and 16-hour days with no overtime pay, and machines are worked 24 hours a day without maintenance and repair. Resources are strained to the breaking point; then, as suddenly as the storm began, it is over—hibernation begins anew for the following month.

Quality suffers in this strange production effort. Soviet goods are marked with production dates; thus when people buy a household appliance, they try to find one stamped with a production date of the 15th or before. If the appliance was made in a storming session, they know it will fall apart very quickly.

A further result of shortages of supplies is the ubiquitous practice of hoarding. Managers make excessive requests to the central bureaucracy for supplies, knowing that the requests will be pruned. Managers keep any superfluous supplies in storage, even when no conceivable need for them can be foreseen. This practice is not as

16

foolish as it sounds. They want goods to trade covertly with other firms for supplies they actually need. Hoarding leads to further inefficiencies and waste—firms seldom have facilities for long-term storage of materials. A *Pravda* editorial chides: "Modern equipment, or formerly modern equipment to be exact, foreign and domestic, sits without use, gets pilfered, and eventually is reduced to scrap metal."[14]

Once managers locate materials, the rigid supply system forces firms to take whatever is allocated to them under the plan. There is no scope to reject goods or discuss needs with suppliers. The manager cannot send back inferior goods, but must either use them in the production process or cut back on production, to the detriment of plan fulfillment.

The experience of the Tashkent Compressor Factory illustrates this universal problem. The factory began producing a piece of cargo-moving machinery that was very well received internationally. However, the plant was limited to producing 250 machines in 1986, far below the demand for the equipment. Chief design engineer A. Vaninsky explained that the factory's suppliers were unable to provide the high-quality, lightweight electric motors required to meet international standards; he cited in particular the defective products of the Baku Electric Machine Manufacturing Factory. But the Tashkent Factory itself was berated for poor-quality goods. In a typical instance, 21 cylinders left the machine shop; only 4 were accepted, while 16 were sent back for reworking and 1 was completely rejected.[15]

In another instance, the Chelyabinsk Electrometallurgical Complex was lagging behind on smelting ferrochrome. The reason was quickly found to be the low-quality lime used in the furnace. But the lime came from the firm itself: The firm's lime-excavating shop was shaving quality to meet its gross output targets, unmindful of the final product.[16]

Although the plan is supposed to be law, up to half of all contracts for the supply and delivery of required inputs are regularly broken

---

[14]*Pravda*, January 8, 1986.

[15]"Ask—And Get No Explanation," letter to the editor, *Pravda*, April 28, 1987, p. 1.

[16]"They Looked at Themselves," *Pravda*, January 14, 1988, p. 1.

between firms. Also, firms commonly lag a year or more behind in fulfilling contractual deliveries. The situation has inevitably led to a breakdown in respect for the law. Managers must break some laws to comply with others. Firms are even ordered by high officials to break laws. Therefore, successful managers are clever swindlers. Never sure when and even if they will obtain materials, they must be adept at finding ways to cheat on fulfilling the plan. An honest manager who tries to run a firm by the book will quickly fail and be replaced by one who does whatever it takes to show results.

Making the Plan

Soviet factory directors must report on the status of the firm's plan fulfillment monthly, quarterly, and annually. Key personnel of the firm spend much of their time preparing these reports. Since the firm's appearance on paper is crucial, the director enlists the aid of the chief accountant, the planning chief, and the chief engineer to manipulate production figures as the deadline approaches and it is clear that the firm is nowhere near fulfilling its norms.

Many methods are used to "improve" the firm's performance on paper. Simulation of plan fulfillment is among the most popular. For example, the management of a state poultry farm that has produced only 70,000 eggs (30 percent under its quota of 100,000), covers its failure by saying that 30,000–40,000 eggs were produced above the 70,000, but those eggs ended up broken or spoiled and were fed to chickens. This phantom production fools no one, but again, the agency responsible for the farm is interested only in numbers. If directors have paper to back up their claims, most likely their supervisors will go along with the scam rather than share blame for failure to fulfill the plan.

This type of fraud is common throughout the Soviet economy and is freely talked about in the press. A. Sukhontsev writes, in a tone laden with sarcasm, that when the tolkach failed to deliver the goods:

> The path to overfulfilled plans, bonuses, and awards was confidently laid by another little word. People pronounced it in a whisper like a terrible incantation, in the darkness, making the sign of the cross:
> "Padded figures."
> It put such fantastic garbage into the computers of the statistical administration that there was no possibility of

> digging down far enough to find the true quantity of crops
> grown and quality of goods produced. Even if someone
> suddenly got a very strong desire to do so.[17]

Today, no one in the Soviet Union places any faith in economic statistics, although the CIA accepted them for many years. Even Gorbachev himself is at a loss to put his finger on accurate figures.

Another popular method of simulating plan fulfillment is to fulfill the overall plan while not achieving the specified assortment of goods. An example is the famous instance of the shoe factory that turned out 100,000 pairs of boys' shoes, instead of the range of men's sizes it was supposed to produce, because it could churn out many more pairs of the smaller boys' shoes from its limited supply of shoe leather. The director was happy, the supervising agency was happy, and Soviet men were out of luck.

Assortment manipulation is rife throughout the Soviet economy, with examples ranging from the fish-processing plants that produce tons of cheap pickled herring in lieu of a specified assortment of fish products to the factories that produce bolts all of one size instead of the assorted sizes needed by Soviet industry. This ever-present problem was depicted in a famous Soviet cartoon of a nail factory that produced its quota in the form of a single giant nail.

Then there is the story of shoe retailers who were convinced to take hundreds of thousands more pairs of women's heavy woolen boots than they could possibly sell. Although demand for boots had been falling, shoe factories did not fulfil their plans for an entire line of women's shoes; they instead concentrated on premium-maximizing boots. During the first year, the Russian Shoe Trade Association (Rosobuvtorg) imposed 10,000 extra pairs on retailers, filling warehouses and stores. The next year the same thing happened, except this time the trade association manager insisted that sellers take 38,300 more pairs of boots, on top of the 13,000 pairs that now languished in storage. When retailers balked, Rosobuvtorg went to local government organizations and told them the provincial trade fair would not be held unless retailers accepted delivery of the additional boots. So shoe sellers ended up with the boots, knowing full well that they could never sell them. The retailers appealed to the provincial organizations to try to stop the

[17]A. Sukhontsev, "Rooster Talk," *Pravda*, January 31, 1987, p. 6.

flow of heavy winter boots, to no avail. At last count, retailers were buried under 200,000 pairs of boots that filled every imaginable space, leaving no room for anything that would sell, but only vague assurances came from the authorities that the flow would stop.[18] This kind of harrowing inanity makes life in the Soviet Union intensely frustrating.

The classic example of the Soviet Union's inability to stop producing outmoded goods is the factory that continued making foot-pedal sewing machines that occupied scarce warehouse space and spilled over into factory aisles. Despite the distribution network's inability to take delivery of any more machines, the plan called for increasing the output.

Production according to gross output targets rather than market demand causes consumers' headaches and producers' nightmares. A factory in a market system would never continue making unwanted goods. If it did, the factory would find that its production cost exceeded the value of its output and it would go out of business.

Another subterfuge used to achieve plan fulfillment is to reduce product quality in order to increase gross output. If a firm has no choice but to accept inferior supplies, it can do little else but use those supplies in production, thereby ensuring the output of defective goods. However, even when firms are able to obtain high-quality inputs, they frequently skimp on materials used in each unit; thus they produce a higher number of inferior goods to achieve plan norms, rather than producing fewer units of quality.

Examples of firms skimping on quality to achieve plan norms are so prevalent that it is difficult to select the most jarring examples from the thousands that would boggle Western minds. One interesting case is the Samarkand Refrigerator Factory, which won numerous red banners for overfulfilling its production plan. But the factory's success does not bear close inspection. While the factory did fulfill its plan for gross output of refrigerators, they were of such dismal quality that most were eventually sent back to the plant—this rejection was in a country where consumers pounce on goods of even subminimal quality. More surprising yet, every year that factory has asked for and received a higher level of subsidy

---

[18]A. Oryol, "Shoes Around the Neck," *Pravda*, September 2, 1986, p. 2.

from the government to produce junk refrigerators that nobody wants.[19]

Examples of shoddy workmanship are endless: New roads collapse, heat pipelines burst in cold weather, floors in new houses look like washing boards, and TVs spontaneously catch fire. Western visitors have reported the astonishing sight of nets extended between the first and second stories of new buildings to catch debris falling from above.

The poor-quality output of one factory becomes the poor-quality input of another, and so on down the line, perpetuating the proliferation of low-quality goods. For example, because of shipments of substandard steel, one factory produces shoddy nails that break when hammered too hard and are unable to withstand standard loads for long periods. In turn, the construction firm that is forced to buy those nails must use them in its building projects. Even in the unlikely event that all other materials meet minimum standards, it does not take much imagination to realize that buildings constructed with these nails are likely to sag and collapse.

Another frequent method of simulating plan fulfillment is to use resources that far exceed the requirements specified in the plan. This approach occurs because managers must use whatever supplies they can find. The gross output system not only causes shortages of all goods, but it can make extremely scarce and expensive goods more obtainable than their cheaper substitutes. The Soviet press has cited numerous instances of heavy-duty materials wasted on production of lightweight goods. Managers are pressed to use the materials or to forgo plan fulfillment.

It is difficult for Western managers to contemplate the scale of waste that results from gross output targets. But if one considers that no enterprise director in the Soviet Union is constrained by a bottom line, that no director faces the specter of bankruptcy if the cost of production consistently exceeds the value of the final product, and that all directors can obtain subsidies from the state banking system to bail out their operations, then it becomes obvious that waste is built into the system. There is no incentive to conserve resources, because the factory manager is determined to meet gross

[19]A. Nikitin, "Where Do Spongers Come From?" *Pravda*, August 30, 1986, p. 2.

21

output targets at whatever the cost. The director knows that the enterprise's financial plan is unimportant in the scheme of things.

Pravda chafes at pipe manufacturers that bury heavyweight pipes in the ground when there are light, heat-resistant substitutes, scolding managers for using the expensive heavyweight metal simply because it is easier to get.[20] In one example, a manager was chastised for plans for oilfield equipment that would contain 25,000 tons of excess pipeline weight. When the pipeline was actually built, however, an inspection showed that more than 75,000 tons of excess materials had been used. Clearly, the director had stumbled on a bonanza of heavyweight materials.

Road construction also falls prey to this affliction. Enterprises insist on surfacing roads with scarce, expensive materials, especially petroleum-bitumen products, instead of using cheaper pressed concrete and local natural rock. Use of expensive surfacing for roads is especially wasteful because of the municipal bureaucracies' habit of tearing up recently completed roads to put in city services and underground communications. According to a workers' proverb, "The road surface is an engineering project that can be done before earth-moving work begins."[21]

Instances of phenomenal waste are common in every sector of the Soviet economy. Piles of wood often rot outside railway stations for want of flat cars to transport them. New piles spring up nearby, to rot in their turn. Expensive trucks rust in the open air, unshielded from Siberian winters, and awaiting delivery of materials scheduled for transport. Economist V. Bolotnova writes of fishing vessels with full holds forming long lines to toss their products back to the sea. He explains that ports cannot handle the catches fast enough. The industrial fishing fleet has expanded annually, while the port industry, processing plants, and ship repair industry lag hopelessly behind.

Also, items such as common household batteries are wasted on a grand scale. Wholesalers insist on taking delivery of consumer electronics products with their power supplies installed. This arrangement would not be so bad if the products were delivered to

[20]"The Optimum Version," *Pravda*, January 9, 1986, p. 2.
[21]Yu. Kazmin, "Wheel in Pothole," *Pravda*, April 24, 1988, p. 2.

the final buyers immediately. But, instead, products sit in warehouses and the installed batteries age, become useless, and have to be written off as a loss. Wholesalers do not care if they have to declare the batteries a loss, because they earned their premiums by fulfilling the plan for products bought. However, hapless consumers cannot make precious electronic goods work even if they are lucky enough to be able to find the products.[22]

Volumes could be devoted to studying the waste of foodstuffs. Despite the consumers' demands for fresh vegetables and fruits, farmers see their produce rot because transporters cannot accept it. Often transporters are overstocked, have no transport cars, and do not have enough storage houses or processing plants. The situation discourages farmers, who end up producing less. The outcome is that even in peak vegetable season, consumers wait in endless lines for scarce produce, while transporters receive their regular salaries for not transporting foodstuffs.

The scale on which human resources are wasted is the most terrible of all. Employees with creative ideas are discouraged from offering their suggestions. The manager is not interested in improvements, because the immediate result would be that the factory would not meet its gross output targets while it was learning about the new method or technology. No one receives prizes or bonuses for inventing a new machine or coming up with a better way to do things. The manager sees that production-oriented innovation does not pay.

Thus, factories use the same outdated equipment and processes for many years, replacing them only when they are hopelessly deteriorated and inadequate. Often, more modern methods and machines are available, but the manager chooses not to use them.

The Soviet press rages against the low technology levels in factories, to no avail. A typical example is the development back in 1955 of a new method for bleaching wood pulp by using oxygen in the manufacture of paper. A rain of studies was produced about implementing the process, but 30 years later the method had yet to be adopted across the industry. Indeed, the test installation at the Amur Pulp and Cardboard Complex became operational only at the end of 1983.

[22]"Batteries in a Bind," letter to the editor, *Pravda*, December 10, 1987, p. 6.

The story worsens when we look at the experience of the Amur Complex. Professor G. Akim, who was one of the original inventors of the process and who by 1986 was quite advanced in age, explained that the installation was fraught with difficulties, such as delays, design errors, and serious shortages of oxygen and parts. "But the big problem," according to Akim, "was that the Amur Complex was in a deep slump; some years it completed only half its planned quota. How can you implement a new idea there?!" Managers failing to fulfill the plan cannot risk falling further behind while the firm retools. In this instance, implementing a technology in the Soviet Union lagged more than 30 years behind Western countries.[23] Many similar cases are described in the Soviet press.

As if Soviet managers do not have enough trouble from external causes, they face serious internal staff problems as well. Such difficulties make up only one part of the director's headaches. Staff morale is low. Wages are a cruel joke. The average Soviet wage does not provide a worker with an acceptable minimal living. Absenteeism becomes a constant headache as workers disappear to conduct personal activities to supplement their incomes, or as they sleep off hangovers from the night before. The workers' proverb states, "You pretend to pay us; we pretend to work." A Moscow manager for a Western airline said that on the days that planes landed, the technical chief would resort to picking up his Soviet mechanics and workers personally to ensure they would be on the job.

Managers cannot count on employees to perform tasks to the best of their ability. Pride in a job well done is almost nonexistent. Workers are not held accountable for their production, because there is no link with the final consumer. Recently, however, there has been talk of changing that lack of connection by instituting trademarks on goods, thereby identifying the producer's factory. Needless to say, plant managers have been less than enthusiastic about the idea, preferring not to have shoddy goods traced to their factory.

Employees are careless about state resources, which essentially have no owners. V. Stepnov describes expensive machine tools that

---

[23]M. Vasin, "But Where Is the Finish Line: The Fate of an Invention," *Pravda*, September 24, 1986, p. 2.

need delicate handling "piled like logs in a stack of firewood"[24] across a factory floor. Dangerous chemicals are carelessly left about on desktops; small items such as nails and screws are strewn about the factory floor. The Soviet factory is a fantastically disorganized, filthy muddle.

The director must also deal with a theft problem so entrenched that workers become known and are contacted for the type of parts they steal. The system itself fosters this antisocial behavior, because the distribution mechanism for resources does not work. Even if a firm wanted to sell superfluous goods to another firm in the official market, firms are prohibited from negotiating transactions directly. Permits authorizing such a transaction could take years. Private individuals step in, stealing goods and selling them to the firm that actually needs them, thereby forming a market outside the law.

The USSR Academy of Sciences reported that "losses of the objects of labor total approximately 70%" and "losses during the use of the means of labor total 40% to 50%."[25] Such figures imply that the Soviet economy operates mainly through theft for sale in the black market.

The authorities vociferously condemn the thieves (while looking the other way) and cynically erect complicated security systems to block intruders from factories, knowing full well that the thieves are on the inside. Everyone knows that the economy would come to a complete stop without the illegal supply system.

For example, Vladimir the bricklayer sells government-owned mortar and bricks to the highest bidder. He pockets the cash so he can bribe the butcher to save choice cuts of meat for him; then he bribes public officials to overlook the shoddy walls he built with substandard bricks not snapped up by the black market. Vladimir is the norm, not the exception. Factory worker Josef steals all the steel girders he can load into the truck that his brother illegally rents from the cooperative manager where he works. Josef pays his brother a percentage of the profits garnered through selling the girders to desperate construction firms. Freezing apartment-dwellers go out on the streets to hail trucks delivering heating oil to a

[24]V. Stepnov, "A Month of Working the New Way," *Pravda*, February 2, 1988, pp. 1–2.

[25]N. Fedorov, "Deputy's Position: According to Incomplete Figures," *Izvestiya*, January 5, 1990, morning ed., p. 2.

factory. They buy oil from the drivers at a high price, who in turn use the proceeds for their own black market purchases. Private enterprise flourishes under a system that was supposed to stamp it out.

Westerners often think that there is a dearth of talent and creativity in the Soviet Union. Nothing could be further from the truth. Soviet managers burst with creativity, but it is misdirected. Their talents are drained in machinations to overcome the irrational system in order to meet their plans. The official system does not work, and none but the most creative could survive in this environment and be successful. There is no reason that boundlessly inventive Soviet managers could not succeed if they were set free to work under a market system. Escaping the discipline of the market has made each manager's life hell and has caused disorganization of production on a grand scale.

The Manager's Political Environment

The official structure of a Soviet firm is set in the supervising ministries by bureaucrats, who are unfamiliar with the day-to-day operations of the firm. The Soviet manager does not have the authority to set or change the organization of the firm. The director, therefore, has had no choice but to accommodate certain people whose functions are outside Western job descriptions.

Among these people are the party secretary of the Communist Party and the chief of the special section. The Communist Party asserts its control over the political beliefs of plant employees through the party secretary. This official sponsors political seminars and conferences at which attendance is often mandatory. Ambitious workers looking for career advancement must dedicate personal time to political activities, rather than to overtime work or strengthening job skills. In addition, party secretaries often butt into the director's business, because their own performance before the party is in part measured by the good performance of the firm.

The chief of the special section represents the KGB at the plant. The chief is given a plan quota to uncover a specified number of spies and saboteurs, regardless of whether any are actually ensconced in the work force. In Stalin's time this official contributed greatly to the terror of the era and to the disorganization of production. Recent reports from respected magazines such as *Literaturnaya*

Gazeta and *Ogonek* suggest that the special section still carries out the same Stalinist era functions, although on a smaller scale. These journals report that workers are still routinely arrested at random, tortured, forced to make confessions, imprisoned, and sometimes even executed—all for no reason: simply because there are planned quotas for crime solutions and sentences.[26]

Although the special section has labored under a reduced plan since the Stalin years, press reports show that the special section chief finds time for other activities. He sometimes functions as a strong-arm bully to quiet consumer criticisms of his firm's shoddy goods. At other times his arrests of saboteurs are a method of firing and reassigning the firm's problem workers. In other instances, he serves as a check on the extent of thievery, and his presence prevents the factory from being stripped and sold on the black market. In yet other cases he may be part of the gangster operation and may prevent honest and naive workers from exposing organized theft.

Soviet managers often complain about the tense, counterproductive working environment arising from the presence of these two officials. At times, active rivalry exists between the director and the party secretary over control of the firm. A party secretary with stronger political connections can often wrest power away from the director. Still, party secretaries can often be counted on in a pinch to use their party connections to get supplies for the firm and, in general, to lend a hand if there is a problem with plan fulfillment. As one former manager put it:

> We were all linked together in life. . . . We were suspicious of each other, but practical life made us work together. In the last analysis we were all subject to the Politburo, he even more than I because he was in the Party.[27]

The career-oriented Soviet manager needs to cultivate and maintain extensive political contacts to survive in this quagmire. Rather than perfecting their management skills, directors spend much of their time in Moscow hobnobbing with the power brokers in the central ministries. The reasons are threefold. First, because managers hold very visible positions, they often become targets of envious

[26]*Literaturnaya Gazeta*, September 24 and December 17, 1986, January 21 and January 28, 1987; and *Ogonek*, February 1987.

[27]Berliner, p. 271.

colleagues bent on their destruction. No laws protect them from anyone who decides to falsely accuse them of a crime against the state. Soviet law places the burden of proof on the defendant. Therefore, the factory director has a pressing need for prominent protectors in the Communist Party.

Second, good political relations are crucial to overcoming the insurmountable obstacles posed by the official system in meeting factory goals. The factory's success hinges on the director's informal network of relationships. Directors who are successful in building political alliances will be able to negotiate more reasonable plans for their factories, plans that are well within a factory's productive capacity. They will also find it easier to get supplies for their firms.

Third, Soviet managers who ingratiate themselves into a circle of powerful cadres will miraculously improve their personal access to the best foodstuffs, imported goods, and most important, good housing.

These three benefits are costly, however. Factory directors must place themselves at the whim of their superiors and influential party members, thereby putting the firm's resources at the disposal of those officials. Managers must drop everything to appease party members, even when those demands interfere with production.

The politicization of economic life is complete. All appointments to important posts require party approval. In 1946 Victor Kravchenko described the milieu in which he had to operate as a factory director:

> Though I had been entrusted with an enterprise running, ultimately, into many millions of government funds, I was not trusted to select my own administrative staff. The top officials were appointed directly by the Commissariat and the chief of Glavtrubostal, without so much as asking my opinion. This system aimed to encourage officials to watch each other and tended to create mutual distrust among people brought together for common tasks. . . .
> From the outset our efforts were snarled in red tape and blocked by bureaucratic stupidity. I had to accumulate materials and tools and arrange for their transport and storage. Thousands of skilled and unskilled workers had to be mobilized, then provided with homes and elementary care. Under normal conditions such problems would not involve insurmountable difficulties. Under our Soviet system every

step required formal decisions by endless bureaus, each of them jealous of its rights and in mortal dread of taking initiative. Repeatedly petty difficulties tied us into knots which no one dared untie without instructions from Moscow. We lived and labored in a jungle of questionnaires, paper forms and reports in seven copies.[28]

Today, managers still struggle to overcome the same irrationalities.

Under Stalin, politics controlled the manager's destiny to a greater extent than today. During the Great Purges, accusations of industrial sabotage were meted out at whim. Managers were routinely sent to the Gulag or shot. Any small mistake could bring the terror apparatus down on the manager's head. Colleagues freely accused colleagues of sabotage, and anyone with a grudge against someone could avenge himself in this way.

Engineer Valentin Bichkov met a typical fate. A competent director of the chemical laboratory at a pipe factory in Nikopol, Bichkov supervised an operation entailing the etching of stainless steel pipe with nitrous acid. A few workers ignored official directions and were overcome by the fumes. Secret police stormed into the factory and dragged Bichkov off to their torture chambers. There was no trial, not even a moment for Bichkov to defend himself from wild accusations that he had deliberately poisoned the workers. In a few days, another hapless engineer entangled in the NKVD (the former name of the KGB) net caught sight of the formerly handsome young engineer: "His face was bruised and swollen. One eye was closed. His overalls—the same ones in which he had been arrested—were torn and bloody. His hands were caked with blood. A foul odor, the odor of prison and illness, hung around him." Bichkov was never seen again.[29]

Even today, managers can still fall prey to such accusations and be subject to arbitrary judgment of their cases and to inhuman punishments. However, these days such treatment is more selective and less brutally applied, with about 1 out of 10,000 people victimized to serve as a warning to the rest.[30] Nevertheless, fear is

[28]Victor Kravchenko, *I Chose Freedom*, reprint (New Brunswick: Transaction Publishers, 1989), p. 328. First published in 1946.

[29]Kravchenko, pp. 266–67.

[30]Bukovsky, *To Build a Castle: My Life as a Dissenter* (New York: Viking Press, 1978), p. 69. Also see *Literaturnaya Gazeta*, September 24 and December 17, 1986, and *Ogonek*, February 1987.

a constant companion and often paralyzes the manager into inaction and buck passing to higher authorities. Turnover is high, because managers can be stripped of their prestigious jobs at the first sign of slipping on plan fulfillment.

In all, Soviet managers experience a level of frustration beyond the experience of their Western counterparts. Kravchenko, who managed the Kemerovo Plant during the Stalin years, described the daily frustrations of his job:

> A few examples may convey the flavor of business under the planlessness which is euphemistically called planned economy.
>
> We were in critical need of brick. . . . At the same time, however, two large and well-equipped brickyards stood idle. They happened to belong to another commissariat which was "conserving" them for some mythical future purposes. I begged and threatened and sent emissaries to Moscow in an attempt to unfreeze these yards, but bureaucracy triumphed over common sense. The brickyards remained dead throughout the period of my stay in the city.
>
> While we were making frenzied efforts to find homes for our workers, a bloc of new houses stood like a taunt, unfinished and useless, on the outskirts of Kemerovo. The credits made available for the project, it appeared, had been exhausted before the work was finished. I had the necessary money to buy and complete this housing but never succeeded in breaking through the entanglements of red tape. The organization which had started the building was willing to relinquish its interest. Everyone, in fact, seemed willing and authorization for the deal seemed about to come through—only it never did.
>
> A vital tramway line running through our area was nearly completed. Several tens of thousands of rubles would have sufficed to put it into operation, and the funds were on tap. But because of some budgetary snarl the city fathers dared not release them without a decision from higher up. I wrote dozens of urgent letters demanding that the line be opened. There were stormy sessions of the City Committee of the Party and the Kemerovo Soviet on the issue. But month after month passed and nothing happened. Meanwhile thousands of weary men and women spent two and three hours a day trudging to and from work.
>
> Such vexations were endless, piled one on the other. They turned every minor task into a major problem. They pinned

down hundreds of useless officials on futile jobs and thus, in a sense, gave them an economic stake in expanding and prolonging the confusions. Every conflict and red-tape blockade, besides, was aggravated by feverish spying, denunciations and investigations.[31]

These days things are still much the same. Only the terror is gone, though arbitrary punishments and the fear they engender are still part of Soviet life.

No Western factory manager can envy the Soviet manager's job. Still, directors of important firms, by all accounts, live like royalty. They receive an excellent salary; a nice, spacious apartment (by Soviet standards); access to special shops in which they can buy the best foodstuffs and imported goods; a splendid country dacha; and innumerable other perks and privileges. But one factory director's wife advised her son to go into another line of work. She said that the job is too stressful and her husband never has a moment's peace. According to her, July is the worst month for her husband; that is when he spends all of his time at the ministry trying to beat down the yearly plan to a manageable level. His constant worry is that the firm's chief engineer, regarded as the ministry's man, will undercut him in negotiations. She also spoke about how the phone never stops ringing at night, with staff calling about bottlenecks and reporting that the metal has not come in from Odessa.

Production to meet gross output targets has made the factory manager's life a nightmare while enforcing scarcity on consumers. But before we examine the deprivation of the Soviet consumer, we need to review why there can be so much production and so little consumption. The gross output target is at fault. It fails to transmit to managers of productive enterprises the information necessary to know if they are making sensible use of the resources. It cannot be overemphasized that producers are disconnected from the final consumer of their goods—the consumer has no impact on production decisions. As long as managers fulfill the plan in terms of gross output, they and their staffs will be rewarded, even though the production is of no use to a consumer.

[31]Kravchenko, pp. 328–29.

Production in the Soviet Union frequently amounts to destroying the original value of the inputs. In the West, we say that the production process adds value to materials. But in the Soviet Union the opposite is often the case. Perfectly good prime materials such as steel, aluminum, and other metals go into producing household appliances that are so poorly made that they cannot be used. Soviet-made goods are virtually worthless on the world market, and the country must export primary commodities such as petroleum, gold, and diamonds to earn foreign exchange. Useless production is the norm in the Soviet Union.

Environmental Destruction

Appalling in itself, production of useless goods is but one disastrous outcome of the Soviet system of gross output production. Another is the destruction of the environment. Unlike American firms, which spend large sums on protecting the environment, Soviet enterprises have had free rein to use national resources without considering costs and to dump wastes wherever they please in their rush to fulfill the plan. As a result, environmental contamination in the Soviet Union is at a level unimaginable in the West. Soviet ecologist M. Ya. Lemeshev laments, "The territory of the entire country is essentially an ecological disaster zone."[32]

Some people are inclined to downplay Soviet pollution in light of our own problems with environmental contamination, but a comparison is in order. The U.S. Environmental Protection Agency (EPA) estimates that each year U.S. industries emit 2.7 billion pounds of toxic chemicals into the air. According to a recent Soviet report, in the Ukraine alone industries discharged 22 billion pounds of toxic substances into the atmosphere during 1988. The 800 million pounds of toxic waste released into the air by a single Ukrainian city, Zaporozhe, which has a population of 875,000, equals about one-third of total U.S. emissions.[33]

The Soviet Union is turning itself into a giant real-life version of Love Canal. Air pollution in 70 cities of the Soviet Union approaches

[32]Yuri Markartsev, "We Have Only One Earth," *Trud*, April 8, 1989, p. 2.

[33]"Nature Requires Protection," *Pravda Ukrainy*, March 25, 1989, p. 3. Also, David Marples, "Ukraine in 1988: Economic and Ecological Issues," in *Radio Liberty Report on the USSR*, Vol. 1, no. 5, February 3, 1989, p. 29.

life-threatening levels.[34] A typical example is the city of Magnitogorsk, where smokestacks of the Magnitogorsk Metallurgical Kombinat belch torrents of exhaust into the hazy sky. Recent measurements show the air contaminated with nine times the legal maximum level of benzene and about four times the legal maximum for sulfur compounds. The population suffers from high rates of heart, lung, and respiratory diseases.

The complex continues production of steel despite the depletion of local iron ore, its remote location, and outmoded technology. The quality of steel has fallen and no longer qualifies for military uses, but relief for the embattled population is nowhere in sight. Plant official Victor Svistunov explains why: "This is a planned system and we've got to provide other enterprises with raw materials."

All major seas and lakes are dying. The Aral Sea of Central Asia, really a lake but called a sea because of its huge size, was once the fourth largest lake in the world. *Izvestiya* reports that in recent years the water level has dropped by 13 meters and the total area has decreased by one-third. Only 40 percent of the water remains. The sea is dying because the rivers that feed it were diverted 30 years ago for irrigation of cotton fields in Central Asia.

As it shrinks, the Aral Sea is becoming saltier. Since 1960, salinity has increased from 10 percent to about 23 percent. The shrinking sea is leaving behind a desert. Sand storms rage in Central Asia, inundating irrigation canals, cotton fields, and cities alike.

Drinking water is scarce; most water goes to the production of cotton. The remaining water is unfit for human consumption, because it is highly polluted by fertilizers. Cancer rates in Central Asia are soaring; in one area of Kazakhstan as many as 261 cases per 1,000 inhabitants were reported.

The entire region of Central Asia may soon be unfit for human habitation. An Uzbek writer asks, "Who can guarantee that a gigantic tragedy will not come to pass in Central Asia and the land will not become uninhabitable?"[35]

---

[34]A. Tsygankov, "The Ecology: Immediate Measures Are Needed," Moscow *Pravitelstvennyy Vestnik*, no. 5, March 1989, p. 9.

[35]"Water for the Aral," *Izvestiya*, May 12, 1989, p. 1. Also Ligachev interview on depletion of Aral Sea, Moscow Television Service, May 13, 1989; and Rusi Nasar, "How the Soviets Murdered a Sea," *Washington Post*, June 4, 1989, p. B3.

Why does this lunacy continue? The answer is that officials are pressed to meet the plan for cotton production, and their prestige and livelihoods depend on gross output of cotton.

The same story is repeated again and again throughout the Soviet Union.

According to a Soviet television documentary, 17 billion gallons of toxic petrochemical waste were released into the Caspian Sea alone during 1988. The huge amount of toxic waste poured into the sea every year is destroying the wildlife. The sturgeon population, source of world-famous Russian caviar, is being exterminated as fish die by the millions. Ecologist V. Sokolov reports that 100 percent of the sturgeon are afflicted with a disease caused by the pollution, and he warns that the unique fish is on the brink of destruction.[36] The concerns fall on deaf ears, however, as the factories bordering the basin still must produce to meet gross output targets. The environmental dangers are ignored in the rush to meet the plan.

The Black Sea, the Baltic Sea, the Barents Sea, and Lake Baikal face the same threat for the same reasons. Millions of dead fish wash ashore, and beaches are awash in sticky black gunk. The fabled Volga and the Dnieper rivers are dying as well, unable to withstand the vast quantities of industrial waste and raw sewage dumped in them each year.

Drinking water all over the country is contaminated. In January 1990, chemicals to cleanse drinking water in Tallinn, the Estonian capital, had not arrived, forcing residents to boil all water. However, even boiling does not make Tallinn's water drinkable, because "without coagulant, the bacteria in the surface water do not precipitate away, nor will mere chlorination make the water drinkable."[37]

Destruction of land is equally appalling. The problem is nowhere as serious as in the Central Chernozem area, which possesses hundreds of thousands of acres of the world's most fertile land. Collective farming strips the land of topsoil. Environmental official F. T.

---

[36]V. Sokolov, article on glasnost in ecology for the UNESCO program "Man and the Biosphere: Ecology and Glasnost," *Izvestiya*, morning ed., March 28, 1989, p. 3. Also, "The Dead Zone," Moscow Television Documentary, Moscow Television Service, May 11, 1989, produced by Azerbaijan Film Studios.

[37]"Railway Problems Affect Cities' Drinking Water," Foreign Broadcast Information Service, January 10, 1990, p. 89.

34

Morgun estimates that the Chernozem soil has lost 50 to 60 percent of its humus. Still worse, iron ore strip-mining operations are carried out in this region, turning large tracts of once-fertile land into an irreversible desert.[38]

Moscow leads the country in overall pollution levels. The Yauza, Likhoborka, and Chertanovka rivers are contaminated with high levels of pesticides, industrial pollution, and sewage. According to ecologist Mikhail Lemeshev, the Moscow River itself "is alive only because we are always adding clean water." The air is fouled by the highest concentration in the Soviet Union of industrial enterprises spewing noxious wastes. Entire forests are dying. On top of everything else, electromagnetic and high-frequency pollution buffets the population. Lemeshev says that over the last 20 years Muscovites' life expectancy has dropped an average of 10 years and residents suffer 50 percent more birth defects than the national average. Moreover, the average Muscovite has two chronic diseases, and up to 75 percent of schoolchildren are sickly.[39]

But even in the capital there is little hope of change for the better. Firms continue to produce to meet plan targets, ignoring environmental hazards. Citizens cannot educate themselves on how much contamination is in their areas because all independent pollution monitoring devices are prohibited in the Soviet Union.

In the Soviet Union, problems often overlap, making conditions even worse for people. For instance, environmental problems may exacerbate ethnic problems; thus Stalin's uprooting of nationalities is coming back to haunt the Communist Party. Recently, in impoverished and despoiled Central Asia, the native Uzbeks and the displaced Meskhets (a tribe whose ancestral home is in Soviet Georgia) fought bloody battles that left more than 100 dead.

Spotlighting Azerbaijan, a region fraught with ethnic violence, a recent Soviet television documentary calls the strife-torn city of Sumgait "The Dead Zone." Footage shows hazardous working conditions in Sumgait's aluminum works, and the narrator reports that Sumgait's air supply is poisoned by 70,000 tons of toxic discharges each year, sickening many of the staff. The film then cuts

[38]Makartsev, p. 2; Kim Smirnov, "19th Party Conference: Tasks of Restructuring: Dictatorship of the Departments or the National Interest?" *Izvestiya*, May 8, 1988, 1st ed., p. 2.

[39]Makartsev, p. 2.

away to show people living in a shantytown among industrial waste. A woman throws a bucketful of slops into a stagnant pond with a crowd of ragged children standing around. More than 20,000 people live in slums in Sumgait, and the area has the dubious distinction of having the highest infant mortality in the country. According to the broadcast, "Some 65 percent of all children are born as blue babies. There isn't enough oxygen in their mothers' wombs. And the results of this are mental handicaps and an irreversible degradation of generations."[40] Hardship conditions such as these stir a bubbling cauldron of ethnic strife.

The Ukraine, a tinderbox of nationalist tensions, is subject to spectacular environmental stresses. The Chernobyl disaster has left large areas uninhabitable for the foreseeable future. Cases of thyroid, mouth and lip cancer, and swollen lymph nodes are already turning up in the disaster's wake. *Moskovskiye Novosti* reports that half the children in one district have thyroid cancer. Four years after the disaster, the authorities have yet to release accurate statistics on radiation levels.

In addition, most rivers and lakes in the Ukraine are dead or dying because of industrial pollution. And 105 industrial and agricultural enterprises dump 10 billion gallons of contaminated water annually into the Dnestr River, the Ukraine's second largest. Pollution is 50 to 100 percent above the norm. Intensive coal mining fouls the Samara River by dumping 5 billion gallons of highly mineralized mine water annually. Drinking water all over the republic is contaminated.[41]

The outbreak of a strange disease in Chernovtsy, a town in the Ukraine, provoked fear and consternation in the population and a wide debate in the Soviet press. In November 1988, 165 children were stricken with infections of the upper respiratory tract, followed by complete baldness. Most doctors contend that the culprit is thallium poisoning. Thallium is a major component of fertilizers.[42]

---

[40]"The Dead Zone."

[41]*Pravda Ukrainy*, December 17, 1988, issue devoted entirely to environmental problems. See also "Solution to Ecological Problems Urged in Ukraine," Kiev *Pravda Ukrainy*, March 25, 1989, p. 3; Makartsev, p. 2; and Marples.

[42]Andrey Borodenkov, *Moscow News* in English, interview with USSR Deputy Minister of Public Health Aleksandr Baranov, no. 13, March 26, 1989, p. 4. (Note: Other possible causes considered by Western and Soviet experts include military-related or radiation sickness.)

In the Soviet Union, industrial accidents occur on a scale unknown in the West. "Lithuania Faces Chemical Chernobyl," "Industrial Accident Poisons Rivers in Chelybinsk," "Toxic Gas Poisoning Hospitalizes 78 Armenians," and "Fire 'Raging' at Estonian Chemical Waste Dump" are just some of the headlines that appeared in the Soviet press in May 1989 alone.

The Soviet Union is on the verge of an ecological breakdown. Prominent biologist and ecologist Alexei Yablokov warned that "there will be disaster," unless the Soviet Union decides to "go green immediately" and undertake drastic measures to improve the environment. He said that 20 percent of the population lives in ecological disaster zones, while an additional 35 to 40 percent live in ecologically "unfavorable areas." According to him, one-third of Soviet men living in these areas eventually get some type of cancer.[43]

The economic system of producing to meet gross output targets has wrought the ecological crisis faced by the Soviet Union. The system protects producers from constraints on their activities as long as they meet their gross output plan. It is useless for planners to insert targets for waste emissions into the plan, because the producer will ignore them to meet the gross output targets, which are more important.

People are organizing into informal groups, which the Soviet press calls the "Greens" movement, to protest environmental disaster. Plans for a fertilizer plant in Odessa were cancelled after protests, and last year local officials were pressured into closing two metallurgical factories in Armenia. To the consternation of the authorities, the informal groups are becoming stronger as the situation worsens, but these groups can, in fact, have only marginal effects while the gross output system remains in place.

In the last analysis, after Soviet factory managers have gone through all of the contortions to fulfill their plans, and in the process ruined the environment, their successes mean nothing for the Soviet consumer. After 70 years of the Soviet system, the consumer still cannot find livable housing; appliances that work; or bread, vegetables, and meat in the stores.

---

[43]"USSR Congress of People's Deputies: Stenographic Record," *Izvestiya*, June 10, 1989, morning ed., pp. 1–11.

3. The Soviet Consumer

> Capitalism, Socialism, and Communism are sitting around talking. Socialism says he needs to do an errand and goes off. Three hours later he returns carrying a small package.
> "What took you so long?" asks Capitalism.
> "I had to buy some sausage, and there was a long line," Socialism explains.
> "What's a line?" asks Capitalism.
> And Communism inquires, "What's sausage?"
>
> —Soviet joke

The producer has gone through his herculean struggle to meet the plan. Bonuses have been distributed, and congratulations handed around. What does this celebration of success mean for the consumer?

Ecstatic headlines in *Pravda* blaring the phenomenal triumphs of the plan would make one think that consumers are jumping for joy: "Steel Production Targets Fulfilled Two Months Ahead of Plan!" and "Plan Overfulfilled by 20%: Refrigeration Plant in Vladivostok Receives Red Banner for 3-Year Performance!" Do consumers cheer? Do they, too, find cause for celebration? No. Consumers can get hardly anything, so it makes little difference to them whether the plan is met or not.

Exploding the Marxist doctrine, prominent economist Nikolai Shmelev announced at the 1989 Congress of People's Deputies that the Soviet Union "exploits its work force more than any other industrial nation in the world," and it pays only 37 percent of its gross national product in salaries. American workers receive 60 percent of the U.S. GNP in wages and benefits. Soviet consumers possess very limited incomes with which to provision themselves. Still, their biggest trouble is not financial.

The fact is that things we take for granted in the United States are nowhere to be found. The consumer has been last on the list

39

with the Politburo since the Bolshevik Revolution. There are no grocery stores piled high with food and household necessities, no stylish clothing shops, no department stores overflowing with merchandise, no drugstores, and no shops at which there is anything of value to buy. Except for a few hours following a delivery, Moscow stores are practically empty. On an average day the perseverant shopper may come up with a moldy jar of pickles and a tin of canned fish after canvassing the city. Soviet citizens cannot grab a quick bite at a fast-food restaurant or pick up bread on the way home from work. Mundane items such as toilet paper and soap elude a protracted search, complicating personal hygiene.

In May 1990, Soviet Foreign Minister Eduard Shevardnadze said that the Kremlin's expansionist, military-first policies throughout the Cold War "made our people, the whole country, destitute."[1] This allocation has meant the neglect of the most basic consumer needs such as housing, food, soap, toothpaste, and toilet paper. Who in the West can imagine nationwide shortages of soap and toothpaste? In our comfortable lives, such "necessities" are taken for granted—as are our food supermarkets.

In America, the greatest hardship one might face while shopping could be finding a parking space close to the store. To Soviet consumers, experiencing an inconvenience of this sort would be sheer heaven. First, to have shops abundant with quality consumer goods is an alien concept for them. Next, to own a personal car is beyond most people's wildest dreams, and finally, to actually have parking spaces for this dream automobile would surely cause the stoutest heart to feel faint. Only 18 households in 1,000 own a car, and as for parking spaces, there is no provision for them, even in Moscow. There are no traffic engineers in the Soviet Union; that profession simply does not exist.

Infrequent shipments of unappealing goods attract long lines of shoppers as if from nowhere. Consumers pounce on overripe vegetables and decaying meat that would be tossed in the trash heap in an American supermarket. Soup bones are a prize find; wilted lettuce, a gastronomic delight. People customarily carry large mesh shopping bags with them at all times, in the unlikely event

[1] In Walter Friedenberg, "Shevardnadze Warns of 'Explosion,'" *Washington Times*, May 7, 1990, p. A1.

that something of value will go on sale. Three or four people standing around a kiosk can precipitate a stampede. People line up first and then ask others what is for sale.

Items such as soap have become so scarce that people regularly form long lines outside stores at the mere rumor that soap, detergent, washing powder, or toothpaste might be on sale. When the country's coal miners went on strike in the summer of 1989, one of their main demands was more soap. Not long ago, two police officers were stabbed when they tried to separate workers fighting over bottles of shampoo.[2]

Buying goods is in itself a complicated process. For example, to buy bread means waiting in line at the cashier's desk in the bread store, paying the exact price in advance, taking a receipt for that amount to the end of a second line at the bread counter and finally handing the receipt to a clerk in exchange for the prized loaf of bread. The same procedure is repeated in every kind of shop for all kinds of goods. To further confuse matters, the stores all close for an hour for lunch, but different kinds of stores close at different times.

Workers, who are jaded from spending two, three, or four hours a day waiting in lines just to buy daily necessities, know that the much-touted perestroika is not working. In fact, obtaining the minimum requirements has become even more difficult under Gorbachev. Consumers are exhausted by the daily struggle to get necessities such as bread, cabbages, sugar, and milk. While the set prices of these items are very low, consumers pay an exorbitant price in loss of time.

Just to obtain milk, for example, Anna, a factory worker and housewife, must take public transportation, time-consuming in itself, from store to store, using her experience to guide her to shops that have received deliveries of milk in the past. A few kopecks here and a ruble placed in strategic hands there will give her tips that she could never have found on her own. One salesclerk tells her about an afternoon milk delivery scheduled for a store on the other side of the city and, made especially garrulous by an extra few kopecks, the clerk advises her how many kopecks she will need

[2]Peter Gumbel, "How Gorbachev's Plan Has Left Soviet Union Without Much Soap," *Wall Street Journal*, November 20, 1989, p. 1.

to bribe another salesclerk to reserve a few liters. Anna immediately rushes to the other store to bribe the clerk before the delivery. Because she is far from the factory where she works, she decides to scour the nearby stores for bread and cabbages while she is there. She keeps an eye out for the milk truck the entire time. Anna manages to get another tip in much the same way about an upcoming shipment of cabbages across town. With that valuable information in hand, she feels the day was productive, although the milk delivery arrived three hours late, precluding her return to work. Once in possession of the valuable liters of milk, Anna carefully arranges them in her shopping bag and presses the bag close to her body to try to prevent the milk from freezing in the subzero temperatures during her long ride home.

If he or she had time to stop and think during the struggle to manage from day to day, the consumer would have to say that life is overwhelmingly difficult. As it is, Anna and millions like her are wrapped up in their efforts to get the next head of cabbage; the next soup bone, which they hope will be less decayed than the last (a child got sick from last week's borscht);[3] and the next loaf of bread. In their scarce free time, consumers plot long-term strategies to buy a carpet for the apartment or a new television to replace the one that burst into flames three months ago while tuned to the evening news.[4] The sheer number of hours Soviets spend in provisioning themselves is staggering.

In an effective international public relations effort, Gorbachev has largely succeeded in winning the support of public opinion in the West, but he has yet to convince his own people that the efforts at perestroika are genuine and that positive change will occur. During a recent trip to Krasnoyarsk, angry Siberians shouted at the General Secretary:

> Go into our shops, Mikhail Sergeyevich. You'll see there's nothing there. . . . We have lines everywhere, for meat, for sausage, for everything. . . . No one's doing anything about housing here. . . . We have no hot water. . . . Our public transport is a disaster![5]

[3]I. Shatunovsky "Eat It Yourself!" *Pravda*, February 9, 1988, p. 6.

[4]"Chelovek i ekonomika," Part 1, interview, *Ogonek*, no. 29, July 1987, p. 5.

[5]Mary Ellen Bortin, "Frustrated Siberians Shout at Gorbachev," *Washington Times*, September 13, 1988, p. 1.

Contrary to the leadership's rosy predictions of economic growth, under Gorbachev and perestroika the Soviet national product has actually declined.[6] Instead of increased production of better-quality goods, stricter quality inspections have merely led to a higher rate of rejecting goods. Fewer goods are on store shelves than before the vaunted program. Vegetables and meat are scarcer than ever, and even bread, which in the past one could always count on finding, must now be tracked by the determined consumer. Sugar and soap are rationed. A Moscow joke states:

> A citizen complains that, according to television reports, the country is producing plentiful supplies of meat, fruit, and vegetables, but when he opens his refrigerator, it is empty. What should he do? "Plug the refrigerator into the TV," he is advised.

People spend endless hours searching for meat. But if they find it, they often risk their health consuming it. At the historic Congress of People's Deputies that convened in 1989, prominent biologist and ecologist Alexei Yablokov reported that 20 percent of all domestically produced sausages contain "life-threatening" substances.[7]

Within the Soviet Union, Mikhail Gorbachev is best known for limiting the sales of vodka in an attempt to combat widespread alcoholism. Consumers used to be able to get vodka easily in state stores; now they must wait in long lines for the opportunity to buy it. A joke expresses public sentiments:

> One man, fed up with the hassles of buying a little nip and of being in a vodka line that never seemed to move, shouted to anyone who would listen: "I'm going to the Kremlin to kill Mikhail Sergeyevich!"
>
> "Bravo, comrade!" others called, as he stalked off.
>
> About an hour later the man was back. A chorus of "What happened?" greeted him upon his return as he took his place again in the queue that had not budged forward an inch.
>
> "That line was twice as long," he said.

[6]Abel Aganbegyan, *The Economic Challenge of Perestroika* (Indianapolis and Bloomington: Indiana University Press, 1988), p. 3.

[7]Yablokov in "USSR Congress of People's Deputies: Stenographic Record," *Izvestiya*, June 10, 1989, morning ed., pp. 1–11.

The average worker, who can slip out of work whenever he or she feels like it, can lose long hours in the ubiquitous lines. Indeed, many workers have little to do until late in the month, because of stalled deliveries of required production supplies. But with most people doing the same thing, no one is on any job. Typically, when a worker runs out of the machine shop to get a shave, the barber has gone to find the shoe repairman, who inevitably turns up at the barbershop to get in line for a haircut.

Professionals, however, cannot spend hours waiting in line. Most women work in the Soviet Union, and married professionals have no time to provision themselves. They must hire someone to do it for them. This person, akin to the tolkach used by companies (in fact, the tolkach often works for private individuals as well), aggressively tracks down supplies. Not just anyone can do this job; success depends upon a huge network of contacts who, through the persuasion of bribes and gifts, keep the professional shopper informed of upcoming shipments of food and consumer goods. This shopping is serious business in the Soviet Union, and the successful person must have, at a minimum, all of the attributes possessed by a top-flight purchasing agent in the West.

The difficulty of obtaining items beyond the basic requirements of life is insurmountable for most. Better-quality food, stylish clothes, costume jewelry, perfumes, shaving cream, and athletic shoes—in sum, all the things that make life more pleasant—simply are not available to the average worker. Unacquainted with small luxuries, Soviet consumers do not miss items that an American would be loath to do without. Their complaints, by and large, concern daily necessities.

The endemic shortage of food angers consumers the most. Even the homeless on the streets of urban America, if they wished, could readily obtain edible cabbages, potatoes, bread, animal fat, sugar, salt, the occasional soup bone, and dairy products—the basic Soviet diet—from the garbage bins of grocery stores. Indeed, the American poor eat much better than this. But recently, consumers in Chelyabinsk watched in frustration as a good harvest of cabbage heads rotted in warehouses. The cabbages had been scheduled for delivery to a distant city, but there were no trucks available to transport them. Rather than break plan orders and sell them to local consumers, farm managers allowed them to rot. Along with many other residents, I. Vasiliev attested that cabbages from the fall harvest were jammed so tightly in Base No. 4, a warehouse, that a bulldozer had to clear them out in the spring. Warehouse workers complained that the blackened cabbages blocked entryways and that they reeled from the stench of the 6-month-old, decayed vegetables.[8]

Even in Moscow, which is much better stocked than the rest of the country, dirty radishes, withered leafy vegetables, yellowed cucumbers, squashed tomatoes, yellowed bunches of dill, and so on are the norm.[9] Only in Moscow's farmers' markets can better produce be found, but at exorbitant prices. Last year, a kilo (about 2.2 pounds) of cucumbers cost eight rubles, or $13.20 at the official exchange rate at the Tula market,[10] and tomatoes were sold at seven rubles a kilo.[11] Because the average Soviet worker earns only 173 rubles per month, such workers can only occasionally consume these vegetables and fruits.

In 1990 the shortages are worsening. Recently, *Izvestiya* called Moscow "the capital of shortages," saying that "it is difficult to imagine now that just recently the whole country used to come here for goods and produce." The newspaper says that the supply of consumer goods "has deteriorated considerably across the whole country," noting that "the shortages in the consumer market pose a practical threat to the very basis of our existence."[12]

From beginning to end, agriculture is a disaster. An acute agricultural labor shortage, coupled with a shortage of capital equipment, ensures that a large portion of crops rots in the fields. Prime Minister Nikolai Ryzhkov puts the loss at 25 to 30 percent.[13] Storage and transport facilities for perishable foods are hopelessly inadequate. Crops are often heaped in open fields because the country lacks proper granaries and warehouses. Most of the remaining harvest

[8]"A Bow from Sponsors," letter to the editor from I. Vasiliev, *Pravda*, April 2, 1987, p. 3.

[9]"Vegetable Counter," letter to the editor, *Pravda*, July 17, 1987, p. 2.

[10]Exchange rate prevailing on January 14, 1988.

[11]G. Yastrebtsov, "Vegetables for Our Table," letter to the editor, *Pravda*, January 14, 1988, p. 3.

[12]I. Demchenko, "Union Gosplan Plan and Realities of Republics," *Izvestiya*, January 27, 1990, morning ed., p.2.

[13]Prime Minister Nikolai Ryzhkov's speech at Council of Ministers meeting, October 1988.

that has survived this treatment is transported to urban areas in open trucks,[14] because refrigerators and refrigerated vehicles are scarce. Opportunities for spoilage are legion.

Moscow, though a city desperate for fresh produce, returns huge quantities of spoiled products to the originating farms. Of the vegetables arriving at the capital city, 10 to 15 percent is sent back. State farms supplying the capital city are inundated with decomposing produce: " 'Returns' are everywhere: Moscow's vegetable supply bases return loads of greens to the farms," proclaim the news stories. Over a five-day period, the Volgograd supply warehouse returned 1,700 kilograms of dill and 620 kilograms of onions to the Mossovet State Farm alone. Newspapers routinely report stories such as this: "The Lyubinsk warehouse returned a ton of dill, a ton of onions, and four thousand bunches of radishes." Scarce labor and equipment to dispose of this waste must be appropriated from productive uses on the farms. The Moscow resident can count on obtaining but few food necessities at state-set prices, among them potatoes.[15]

Production of processed foods fares no better. Attempts by Soviet factories to make quality foods have met with abject failure. One bite of the Tyumen Factory's chocolate cookie, which according to Soviet journalist I. Shatunovsky cannot be chewed without "the use of gear-cutting machines and special pulverizers," should convince any doubter. If the cookie is unconvincing, the still-intrepid gourmand could sample rotting, maggot-filled sausage courtesy of the Arkhangelsk Meat-Packing Plant,[16] or cans of corned beef, described by a Western visitor as "very corroded on the inside, with black spots."[17] Also available, after a long wait in line, are boiled "milk sausage" with filler that decomposes into "a slippery piece of soap" after a few days in the refrigerator; a strange substance called "sandwich butter," which is half real butter and half a whitish material;[18] tea that has tiny wooden branches and other

[14]"Vegetable Counter."

[15]"Vegetable Counter."

[16]Shatunovsky, p. 6.

[17]"Soviet Union: Not Exactly a Workers' Paradise," *The Economist*, February 28, 1987, p. 49.

[18]Vladimir Prokushev, "Only a Line Is Guaranteed," *Pravda*, February 2, 1988, p. 2.

leaves mixed with tea leaves; curdled sour cream; and darkened, blotched chickens emitting a stench inherent to decomposing poultry, among other treats.

With so much unsavory food, the reader should not be surprised to learn that food poisoning is common in the Soviet Union. Mass poisoning, especially poisoning caused by spoiled canned fish and milk products, is frequently reported in the Soviet press.[19] In addition, workers often become sick from food at cafeterias, where they usually eat one meal a day. Cleanliness is nonexistent in cafeterias and restaurants. Grease and dirt are permanently caked onto kitchen facilities, and cooking implements are rarely clean either. Kitchen workers themselves are unconcerned about personal hygiene. Soviet leaders are very concerned about the problem of food poisoning, which they consider in the context of health care.

A café on Rustaveli Avenue in Tbilisi, Georgia, although stocked with some meats and fruits, is otherwise typical of Soviet restaurants. According to a Western visitor, "The roof leaks, and the plaster on the ceiling and walls is blotched with damp. Large windows along the front wall are coated with greasy dirt. Along the back wall, light fixtures hold bare bulbs, also coated with grease and grime." Customers sit at small formica tables. After sampling the food and drink, the visitor remarked, "It [a wine cocktail] came with pieces of apple and a cherry floating in it, and tasted of fruit juice. A second one, ordered 20 minutes later, had neither apple nor cherry, and tasted entirely different. Dinner (roast chicken) was served with a makeshift variety of utensils, including feather-light aluminum cutlery. The waitress apologized, but she couldn't serve any coffee—all the cups were in use."[20]

Fresh meat is rarely available anywhere in the country and almost never in state stores in rural areas. Occasionally, Moscow residents will find soup bones and inedible-looking frozen meats. Rarely can they indulge their cravings for sausage, a traditional food. Fresh fish is unheard of.

One Western visitor saw a remarkable sight in Tashkent. When people spotted a meat truck, buses veered off their regular routes

[19]Shatunovsky, p.6; also *TASS*, May 20, 1989, on Uzbek paratyphoid cases.

[20]Robert G. Kaiser, *Russia: The People and the Power* (New York: Washington Square Press, 1984), p. 70.

and followed the meat. As the delivery truck approached the meat shop, passengers stormed out to form lines. Cars and passersby also converged on the scene. A long line was waiting before the meat was carried in.

Khrushchev's memoirs contain this story of his encounter with a man on the street:

> "Say, Comrade Khrushchev, do you think a camel could make it all the way from Moscow to Vladivostok [a trip of more than 6,000 miles]?"
>
> I could tell from the way he was smiling that there was more to the question than met the eye. I answered cautiously, "Well, the camel is a strong animal with lots of stamina, so I think he could probably walk all the way to Vladivostok."
>
> "No, Comrade Khrushchev, you're wrong. The camel would be lucky to make it as far as Sverdlovsk [about 1,200 miles east of Moscow]."
>
> "Why?"
>
> "Because, assuming he gets to Sverdlovsk, the people there would eat him."[21]

New Year's Day, the most eagerly anticipated holiday on the Soviet calendar, was a grim disappointment in 1989. Consumers hunted in vain for salami and cheese, chicken, cakes and sweets, coffee, tea, sugar, and yeast to prepare the traditional feast. Gifts of children's clothing, boots, perfume, and toys were hard to come by; bath soap, laundry detergent, meat, butter, and sugar were rationed in many cities. Only the most energetic housewives, by pounding the steets and bribing their way weeks in advance, were able to come up with some semblance of a festive meal.

The Soviet consumer spent a poor holiday compared to most residents of the Third World, who manage to throw a party for the biggest holidays, even on very limited incomes.

Cities in the Soviet Union are ranked in order of importance and are provisioned with consumer goods and transportation networks accordingly. Life is by no measure easy in the main cities, but in provincial cities it is harder still. A resident of Akhtyrka, a regional center in Sumy Province, complains that food shops are bare and

[21]Nikita Khrushchev, *Khrushchev Remembers: The Last Testament*, translated and edited by S. Talbott (New York: Little, Brown & Co., 1974), p. 143.

even the farmers' cooperative shop is empty. Roads are a mass of potholes and bumps, ditches and mud. Most residents live in small houses with little access to amenities, and most heat their homes and cook over a wood-burning stove. Only multistory apartment buildings in the city's center have modern conveniences such as gas heat and relatively dependable electricity.[22]

Manufactured Goods

Manufactured goods, produced under the aegis of the Ministry of Light Industry, are scarce and of poor quality. State companies churn out hair dryers that short-circuit, vacuum cleaners that do not work, refrigerators without motors, sewing machines missing one small screw essential to their working, and primitive washing machines that do no more than get clothes wet. Desperate consumers snap up anything they think they can somehow make work.

Televisions, an item that many people can obtain after an arduous search and a number of bribes, have a peculiar habit of bursting into flames and, in the process, burning down houses. Abel Aganbegyan, economic adviser to Gorbachev, remarked that more than 2,000 color televisions catch fire yearly in Moscow alone.[23] Recently in the Soviet press, an article promoting new televisions drew attention to this widespread problem by trumpeting the following among the list of the new sets' virtues: "The possibility of the set catching fire is reduced to a minimum."[24]

Telephones are in short supply everywhere, and are practically nonexistent in rural areas. In the major cities people wait many years for telephone service. *Pravda* writer V. Prokhorov points out that of all the lines accompanying Soviet consumers from cradle to grave, the line for home telephone installation is one of the longest:

> Some people wait years, even decades for this splendid means of human communication, as if awaiting a miracle. And while a young and strong person may start the telephone marathon, he may reach the finish line a veteran

[22]"After All, It's a Regional Center," letter to the editor, *Pravda*, January 12, 1987, p. 7.

[23]"Chelovek i ekonomika," p. 5.

[24]"We're Buying a TV Set," *Pravda*, February 28, 1988, p. 3.

49

hoary with age, for whom the bell may have already rung, even without a telephone.[25]

Once installed, telephone service breaks down often. In the city of Volgograd, 400 repair requests were recorded for each 100 telephones. When asked why there is such a problem with repairs, communications officials responded with outlandish explanations to cover the truth about poor-quality telephones and telephone lines. They claim consumers mistreat the telephones—they bang down the receivers, grandparents let their grandchildren play with the phones, etc.[26]

However, it is easy to find junk goods, if one is so inclined. Warehouses contain vast stores of unsalable goods. Managers would pay people to take the junk off their hands, but there are no takers. For example, several million rubles worth of handkerchiefs, which better deserve the name of rags because they are made of rough-texture, low-quality cotton cloth, accumulate in warehouses. Consumers clamor for well-made handkerchiefs, but the Pavlovsky Posad Association continues to churn out the useless variety.[27]

Consumers' complaints to authorities about the poor quality of consumer goods are useless, or worse. Examples abound in the Soviet press. One hapless woman bought a down comforter. In the winter when she tried to use it, the down and feathers came out through the covering. She sent the comforter back to the Kotovsk Down and Feather Factory to be replaced. She did not receive the hoped-for response. Instead, the factory wrote a nasty letter accusing her of abusing the comforter and causing the stuffing to come out. *Pravda* correspondent A. Golovenko says that this kind of response is very common; a factory director can "beat off any 'nonscientific' complaint sent by a simplehearted buyer as if it were a piece of fluff. All he has to do is accuse the buyer of not following the instructions for using the item." Factories use this dodge to avoid meaningful responses to people sending back every kind of good: worthless radio receivers and cameras, watches and tape recorders, shoes and automobile tires.

[25]V. Prokhorov, "Telephone Marathon," *Pravda*, March 20, 1987, p. 3.
[26]V. Stepnov, "No Chance to Get Through," *Pravda*, March 6, 1987, p. 3.
[27]"Supply and Demand," *Pravda*, September 10, 1987, p. 1.

One unsuspecting provincial television owner took his set to the deputy minister. Why does the screen go blank? Where's the sound? The TV owner thought he was doing an important service by informing the minister that there were problems, but he was in for a shock. Company officials were present and declared the complaint to be unscientific, because he should have known it is impossible to turn out a TV set that works perfectly.[28]

In the Soviet Union, the lucky few who have cars run into another set of frustrations. The February 1989 issue of the U.S. magazine *Car & Driver* tells of a Soviet photographer who waited one year to have his car booked into a shop for repairs. After the car had sat in the shop for three months, the desperate owner finally resorted to a hunger strike to convince the shop to repair his car next.

Production of consumer goods, like everything else, is seemingly uncoordinated. Factories produce goods to be delivered to distant provinces while using production inputs from equally faraway suppliers as designated by the supervising ministry. This policy leads to terrible inefficiencies and waste. The Noginsk Sewing Factory, located in Moscow Province, makes thermal suits for workers in the Taiga; to make the suits, Noginsk workers use wristbands sent in from the Cheryomkhovo Sock Factory across the continent in Irkutsk. The Noginsk Sewing Factory has to halt completion of the suits while it waits six months to a year for deliveries from Irkutsk. Yet a factory in Noginsk makes the very same wristbands, but the sewing factory is forbidden to use them; those bands are destined for a far-off buyer.[29] Needless to say, poorly clothed workers in the Taiga wait years for delivery of their suits.

Soviet leaders consciously planned this far-flung production process. They wanted all areas of the country to be completely interdependent, thereby limiting the power of local leaders and ensuring that all republics remain totally subservient to Moscow.

Housing

To add to the consumers' frustrations, they come home to tiny, badly constructed, and poorly maintained apartments. Housing is supplied by the government, which has decided that everyone

---

[28]A. Golovenko, "Coverlet Made a Run for It . . . , " *Pravda*, September 5, 1987, p. 3.

[29]Letter to the editor, *Pravda*, July 7, 1986, p. 7.

should live in grim, dingy, high-rise apartment buildings. Workers do not have the option to decide for themselves where they will live and how much space they need.

A severe shortage of apartments has been endemic to the Soviet economy since its inception, for the military build-up always received priority over production of consumer goods, including housing. The dearth of apartments prevents young couples and singles from starting their own households, forcing extended families to share a cramped space. Domestic battles rage in the tight living quarters. A recent survey attributed 11 percent of divorces to the severe housing crunch.

Soviet statistics put per capita living space at about 97 square feet in Moscow, and 75 square feet in the rest of the country. We believe these figures exaggerate, as reports from the Soviet Union invariably refer to tiny, cramped apartments, but according to this norm the average worker, if very lucky, has a two-room apartment to house four people.[30]

Soviet consumers are not consoled by the fact that housing is comparatively very cheap. Rent typically takes only about 5 percent of the family budget (compared with 20 to 30 percent in the West), but all they get for their money is cramped, unsanitary cubicles. Only the small elite can obtain better apartments using their high-level connections and a large supply of rubles to bribe their way to a higher priority on housing waiting lists. Once the privileged get their apartments, however, they still pay the same low rent as the inadequately housed masses.

The two-room apartment that a Muscovite would be thrilled to have is usually divided into two areas: living and sleeping. Typically, a small cooking stove, small refrigerator, kitchen table, chairs, and inferiorly made couch are squeezed into one room. Cooking implements hang from walls and are stowed in ingenious makeshift storage cabinets. An entire family's sleeping quarters are crammed into the other room. Flimsy bureaus, often made of cardboard or low-grade wood, contain clothes and family belongings. All available space is used, with storage space invented out of unlikely

[30]*Argumenty i Fakty*, no. 32, 1988, p. 5., estimates that per capita square meter space now averages nine square meters. Also see Henry Morton, "Housing Quality and Housing Classes in the Soviet Union," in *Quality of Life in the Soviet Union*, edited by Horst Herlemann (Boulder: Westview Press, 1987), p. 95.

corners, below ceilings, and under beds. Privacy is nonexistent. These are the conditions to which Soviet consumers aspire, and large numbers of them do not live this well. For many, this apartment is their biggest dream, obtained only after years on a waiting list.

Construction crews leave new apartment buildings unfinished. Families that move in must connect the plumbing and electricity themselves, find window glass and pay someone to install it,[31] finish ceilings, and somehow get details such as bathroom fixtures and paint. Desperation for an apartment is so great, however, that people are happy to finish the work of the construction crews, knowing that they are now among the lucky ones with a little more space.

Soviet apartments are junk to the Western eye and, indeed, to Soviet apartment-dwellers themselves. It is impossible to distinguish new Soviet-built buildings from older ones. New buildings are subject to "instant aging." Inside and out, materials begin wearing out immediately: New buildings visibly sag; inside walls, floors, and ceilings sag; cracks appear; plaster and dust rain down; walls are a dingy gray; and chunks of concrete loosen from the building. Inferior nails (ubiquitous in Soviet construction) break, at best causing only minor annoyance such as doors coming unhinged. Floorboards are rough and unfinished and splinter easily. Walls are either too thin, raising the noise level and putting the ceiling in danger of collapse, or too thick, endangering the floor and the apartment below. Apartments do not have handy amenities such as closets and kitchen cabinets that Americans take for granted. Roofs invariably leak and heating is sporadic.

In addition to dangerous construction, Soviet apartment-dwellers must cope with heating problems. *Pravda* correspondent N. Bratchikov asserts that a large number of apartments in the Siberian city of Vladivostok have been without heat for many years. Many apartment walls there are covered with frost throughout the winter.[32] In the city of Ust-Labinsk, residents complained about the scarcity of coal to burn in their home stoves. One couple protested that they needed at least one and a half tons of coal to heat their home per

[31]"Stolen Time," *Pravda*, January 8, 1987, p. 3.
[32]N. Bratchikov, "Who Heats the City?" *Pravda*, January 9, 1987, p. 3.

season, but they could get only a third of that, after an arduous process that they described:

> This year you have to go to the technical inventory office first to get a form about how much living space you have. . . . Then you have to visit the regional executive committee to fill out a fuel booklet there. Then you have to go to the regional fuel department. But they won't give you the form you need there until you pay them 10 rubles "for inventory taking" (which virtually hasn't been done for almost 15 years). It's a real marathon for an invalid.[33]

According to the couple, coal rations were so low because city officials, eager to fulfill the plan for gas heat, fraudulently reported that the city had completely switched to gas heat and thus needed less coal.

Only about two-thirds of Soviet apartments have running water, and just one-third have hot water.[34] Even in those apartments, water is frequently unavailable, and when it is, it often comes out a brownish color. In short, Soviet apartments are subject to all the failures of the larger society.

But the extraordinary hardships of the two-room apartment would be heaven for one-fifth of the Soviet population. According to Soviet estimates, 20 percent of the population still lives in communal apartments, an awful type of housing created by partitioning buildings. One Muscovite who later obtained a better apartment said:

> Communal apartments were like a hotel corridor, twelve rooms opening out, four or five people living in each room, endless arguments about who would sweep the corridor today. You had to wait half an hour to urinate; you couldn't bathe; there were horrid smells, people washing, cooking all the time, no privacy.[35]

Only one bath and one kitchen served all 12 rooms, a total of almost 60 people.

[33]The Moiseevs, "Forms, Forms," *Pravda*, September 5, 1987, p. 2.

[34]Mikhail Bernstam, "The Collapse of the Soviet Welfare State," *National Review*, November 6, 1987, p. 40.

[35]David K. Shipler, *Russia: Broken Idols, Solemn Dreams* (New York: Viking Penguin Inc., 1987), p. 175. First published in 1983.

Others, especially newcomers to a city, must make do by renting a "corner" of a room that has been divided into quarters by hanging sheets. Four separate people or couples live in one room. Alternatively, they must find space in a dormitory or barracks sheltering 5 to 20 people per room.[36] I. Boginsky complains that, at best, newly arrived teachers in the Ukrainian city of Dnepropetrovsk must go to a dormitory after school, where the school intercedes and gets them beds. At worst, they end up in a corner of an apartment rented from an enterprising tenant.[37] Invariably, someone renting a corner of an apartment pays more to the tenant for that tiny space than the tenant pays for the whole apartment.

In the provinces, the picture is much worse. Housing needs are cruelly neglected for workers in Siberian mining areas that face winter temperatures of −50 degrees Celsius. Funds are invested to expand production of molybdenum and gold in Chita Province, but nothing is spent to make life better for residents. Anatoly Krivitskikh, an ore dredger, lives in a corner of an apartment in a poured-slag building that freezes and cracks in cold weather. Still, he is happy to have that, because dozens of families in the settlement are living in tents and holes in the ground, making do however they can with little protection against the cold. The workers' dream in Chita Province is to have a tiny room in a standard five-story unit built according to designs many years old. None of the buildings have heat or water, and sewage is dumped untreated in the local river.[38]

Families in Chita exist in misery, exposed to the cold while living in a forest. Why not chop some trees and build their own houses? Because the timber industries export the lumber to other regions and will sell it to residents only at very high prices. Worse yet, residents must stand passively by and watch while thousands of cubic meters of wood are wasted as a result of backward felling practices. They must breathe the acrid smoke of gigantic bonfires of wood waste that could have been put to use. In addition, other materials are not available in the region and have to be sought out and hauled in by rail—slate, roofing felt, glass, bricks, pipes,

[36]Bernstam, p. 40.

[37]"Teachers' Dormitory," letter to the editor, *Pravda*, January 26, 1987, p. 7.

[38]B. Mironov, "In One Word: Shame," *Pravda*, January 22, 1988, p. 3.

radiators, everything—a very expensive endeavor.[39] Conditions prevailing in Chita Province are symptomatic of provinces across the country.

The official housing statistics present a grim picture, but the reality emerges as truly abysmal when one takes into account the fact that the official data suffer from the same kinds of gross manipulations and lies that affect all Soviet statistics. For example, authorities estimate that in the 1960s, 60 percent of the population lived in communal housing and that the number declined to 20 percent in the late 1980s. In the first place, probably much more than 60 percent of the populace lived in communal housing in the 1960s— perhaps as high as 85 percent. Soviet official statistics always understate problems; the difficulty is in figuring out by how much. Next, when one takes into account massive military spending, which has accelerated during 73 years of Bolshevism and continues to the present, and when one contrasts it with an admitted 20-year economic performance of little or no growth,[40] a reorientation toward the housing sector on a large scale clearly did not happen. The upshot is that a large sector of the population still lives in communal housing and has been awaiting new apartments for decades.

Medical Care

Medical care is allocated the same way as everything else in the Soviet Union: according to plan. Plan norms that lead to shoddy production and shortages in other sectors of the economy take on a sinister new meaning when applied to the health of individuals.

Different systems of medical care serve different classes of people in the Soviet Union. Persons high in the party hierarchy have access to a high-quality closed system of medical care, while nonmembers with low-status jobs—the vast majority of the population—do not. Within the closed system, there are also gradations. The higher one is in the hierarchy and the better connections one has, the better medical care one receives within the closed system.

[39]Mironov, p. 3.

[40]Communique on the Plenary Session of the Central Committee of the Communist Party of the Soviet Union, *Pravda* and *Izvestiya*, February 18, 1988, p. 1. Also, Daniel Franklin, "The Soviet Economy," *The Economist*, April 9, 1988; and Abram Bergson, "Gorbachev on Soviet Growth Rate," Radio Free Europe/Radio Liberty, March 25, 1988.

Average Soviet workers receive medical care in the district where they live, or if they are lucky, they may have access to the lowest level of the closed system of medical care through the factory where they work. The first duty of medical staff members is to please their supervising agency, which oversees plan fulfillment for the hospital or clinic. Patients' needs are a distant second.

The medical profession does not enjoy the high prestige in the Soviet Union that it does in the West. Doctors and nurses are extremely underpaid and refuse to give adequate care without bribes to supplement their low salaries. Patients are denied food and treatment if they do not pay the bribes. One woman who went through a kidney operation said, "A ruble to the nurse gets you a thermometer, another gets the sheets changed, another the toilet cleaned." She added, "The surgeon gets a hundred or you'll just wait in bed. The chief physician already took a hundred to admit you to a clean ward."[41] Patient care is generally very brusque and unfeeling, unless a large amount of money changes hands. Nursing is looked down upon in the Soviet Union; therefore, there are few highly trained, professional nurses.[42]

Hospitals and clinics are assigned quotas to fulfill for numbers of operations performed, hospital beds built per year, numbers of patients seen, deaths per year, and so on. If a hospital is running short on its quota for appendectomies or tonsillectomies, for example, doctors may resort to performing unnecessary surgery on patients receiving other operations in order to fulfill the plan. Even when doctors' actions do not get that out of hand, the pressure runs high for a doctor, who is examining a patient, to diagnose an ailment curable by a procedure currently falling short of plan fulfillment. A quota sets a limit on the number of deaths allowable at the hospital per year. The authorities will investigate hospital practices if deaths per year exceed the quota. This norm has the effect of excluding the terminally ill from hospital care as doctors compel families to take those people home to die.

Each operation also has a fixed hospital stay that is called for in the plan and that must be fulfilled. Delivery of a baby is usually set

[41]Mark D'Anastasio, "Red Medicine: Soviet Health System, Despite Early Claims, Is Riddled by Failures," *Wall Street Journal*, August 18, 1987, p. 1.

[42]Mark G. Field, "Medical Care in the Soviet Union," in Herlemann, p. 76.

at 9 days; an appendectomy, 10 days; and a hysterectomy, 14 days. Patients well enough to be discharged earlier are forced to stay the entire period.[43]

Facilities for the effective treatment of serious illnesses such as cardiopulmonary conditions and cancer do not exist outside the closed system of medical care. Ordinary citizens often do without any treatment at all or receive placebos that do not treat the problem. Average citizens have difficulty obtaining aspirin, never mind the expensive drugs needed to treat a heart condition. At best, if the sick person lives in a major urban area and has a large supply of rubles, he or she may be able to pay the large sums required for a doctor or surgeon and for medication obtained on the black market.

The pharmaceutical industry in the Soviet Union, like all industries in the country, must produce medicines according to a plan. The quotas are set high, but the available supply of input chemicals is very small. To achieve plan fulfillment and get premiums for good performance, factories stretch scarce materials, leading to the production of weak and useless drugs. Consumers are especially leery of above-plan production of drugs (undertaken by the factory for maximum premium rewards). Such drugs rarely contain anything more than sugar or salt and water. If a medication does not work, consumers say it was "above-plan production." Needless to say, a thriving black market exists with sky-high prices for imported medicines.

Medical staffs spend an inordinate amount of time on paperwork. They must coordinate each procedure and diagnosis with numbers specified in the plan. And when, despite maneuvers and compromises with patient health care, these numbers do not match up, they resort to documenting fictitious operations, reporting construction of nonexistent hospital wings, and in general falsifying statistics to meet the plan.

Hospital conditions are terrible. Wards are overcrowded, unsanitary, and sloppy. Shortages are endemic for everything from medicines and medical supplies to food and cleaning supplies. Modern medical equipment is exclusively reserved for the closed medical system. District hospitals and clinics do not possess the equipment

43Field, p. 72.

and medicines to treat life-threatening illnesses. Even basic equipment such as sheets, towels, bandages, and adhesive tape is scarce. According to Soviet Health Minister Yevgeny Chazov, more than a third of district hospitals have no hot water, and 27 percent have no sewerage. Soviets dread a hospital stay; conditions are much like those prevailing in hospitals in the West a century ago. Infection runs rampant, and it is easy to see why. Poor sanitation and lack of disposable items such as gloves, thermometers, syringes, needles, intravenous tubing, and catheters provide an excellent breeding ground for disease.

Dr. Kenneth Prager of Columbia College of Physicians and Surgeons in New York recounts an encounter in the Soviet Union with an 80-year-old man in great pain from a prostate condition:

> His bladder was markedly distended and he obviously needed to be catheterized immediately. The urologist who had been summoned to his home complied with my request for a rubber glove to examine the patient's prostate gland. After examining him, I was startled when the physician requested that I wash the glove so that it could be reused. She then relieved the patient of his distress by passing her only, reusable catheter into his bladder after lubricating it with butter. She had sterilized the catheter by boiling it in a pot of water in the patient's kitchen.[44]

The Botkin Hospital in Moscow is among the better hospitals, because Westerners are sometimes hospitalized there. But an American citizen who was hospitalized at Botkin reports:

> There were three toilets for 76 men. These had no seats, and unless one brought along a morning copy of *Pravda*, no toilet paper. Compounding the problem, Soviet hospitals dispense enemas as readily as American hospitals give back rubs. Hospital toilets always seem to be in use, and they frequently overflow, covering bathroom floors with a sticky mixture of urine and feces.[45]

The situation in provincial and rural hospitals is worse. Plumbing is a prized commodity; adequate heating, a luxury. A. Kostikova

[44]Kenneth M. Prager, "Soviet Health Care's Critical Condition," *Wall Street Journal*, January 29, 1987.
[45]Field, p. 77.

and others report that many hospitals in Andizhan Province are overflowing with patients; beds are everywhere, including hallways. As a result, hospitals can never be disinfected or closed for repair. Supplies such as respiratory equipment, anesthesia, and even beds, hot-water bottles, and tape measures are scarce. Also, the level of staff training is so low that "things have reached the point that certain young doctors are unable to make an injection into a vein and are unable to deal with elementary questions of treatment, not to mention their skills in operating."[46]

Residents of Itaka, a mining town in the Taiga region, must somehow get by with a three-ward "hospital." *Pravda* correspondent B. Mironov reports:

> A curtained-off corner with three beds—that's the men's ward. Behind the same sort of cheery chintz curtains is another ward, with one bed more than the first—this is the combined women's and children's ward. The third ward— the maternity department—stands behind a plywood door. And what about equipment?
>
> "We don't have any," hospital manager N. Komleva sighed heavily. "All we get is syringes—we don't even have scales for the pregnant women."[47]

The regional hospital is similarly lacking in facilities. The institution is understaffed by half and has not had an oculist or ear-nose-and-throat specialist since 1972. Patients requiring these specialists are sent to the capital of the republic, Chita, which is 18 to 20 hours away by train. Once patients get there, however, no accommodations are waiting for them and no help is forthcoming, so they often simply turn around and go home. The central government is doing worse than nothing about the problems, for it has slashed the region's medical budget. Plans for a water purification plant have been scrapped. Meanwhile sewage pours into the nearby river, causing epidemics of jaundice and dysentery that are halted only with the onset of cold weather.

Winter temperatures of −50 degrees Celsius bring on their own set of ailments. Because families lack appropriate housing, they are

[46]A. Kostikova et al., "Beyond the Pale of Decisions," *Pravda*, February 7, 1987, p. 3.

[47]Mironov, p. 3.

exposed to the cold and suffer severe respiratory diseases, which area hospitals do not have the facilities or medications to treat. Death rates are high.

In addition, environmental contamination is a severe problem in the mining and industrial areas. Mironov attests that large numbers of people in the Transbaikal mining region suffer from fluorosis, goiter, Urov disease, molybdenum gout, and other serious conditions caused by the presence of fluorine, mercury, and molybdenum in the environment. Sufferers cannot get treatment for these conditions.[48]

The regional hospital located in Mogocha, an important molybdenum mining town in the Taiga, is impoverished. There is no plumbing—the hospital water supply is trucked in, and for toilets patients must use an unheated outhouse, facing winter temperatures of below −50 degrees Celsius. A new one-story clinic cannot open because it lacks iron radiators for hot-water heating.[49] A *Pravda* correspondent reports that radiators cannot be found anywhere in the entire province.

Medical practitioners frequently cling to outdated ideas. For instance, the belief persists that infection is brought into the hospital from outside. Hospital visitors must leave their coats in another room and cannot put books, flowers, or gifts of any kind on a patient's bed for fear of contamination. A Western visitor reports:

> Such meaningless rules are ferociously enforced, while sterility is poorly observed in operating rooms despite the fact that most infections originate within hospitals. As a result, the incidence of postoperative infection is very high, affecting about one-third of all patients.[50]

Overcrowding in hospitals is truly extraordinary. One Soviet surgeon noted:

> Beds are jammed into corridors, sometimes so tightly that there is no room to pass through. Beds are put next to the elevators, next to the dining rooms. I remember one case when a nurse couldn't find a place for a patient anywhere, and ended up putting him on two tables in the dining room

[48]Mironov, p. 3.
[49]Mironov, p. 3.
[50]Field, p. 72.

that she pulled together. The next morning other patients came in for breakfast, saw this makeshift arrangement, and refused to eat. It was a big scandal. A commission came to investigate it.[51]

Soviet medical care ranks below that of many Third World countries. Soviet Health Minister Yevgeny Chazov announced in August 1988 that the Soviet Union has a dismal record of infant mortality with 25.4 deaths per 1,000 live births, placing the Soviet Union 50th in world ranking. In reality, the rate is much higher and the truth, much bleaker. An investigation turned up numerous instances of cover-ups of children's deaths in the Moscow region, raising the official number for the area by 300 percent.[52] Even in Moscow, women and children are lucky to escape from hospitals with their lives.

In the provinces, infant mortality is much worse. In a related investigation, a figure of 55 deaths per 1,000 people appeared in *Pravda* for Surkhandarya Province. The truth is still bleaker. In an example of an everyday occurrence, eight newborns died of toxic septic disease in a city hospital of Sovetabad. Basic sanitary standards were ignored. Staff members neglected to ensure the cleanliness of the formula, even after the first baby died. The hospital administration then tried to cover up the deaths. In another instance, a woman brought a sick infant into the Termez Central Regional Hospital. The baby was diagnosed with acute intestinal illness, but then everyone forgot about the child, and no tests were done for five days. The only doubt about the fate of that child is whether or not the death was included in mortality statistics. Examples abound in the Soviet press of inappropriate diagnoses, improper medication, and sheer negligence causing infant deaths.

Other death rates have soared as well. Soviet sources now place the average male life expectancy at 65 years,[53] compared to 71 years in the United States. Unofficial Soviet sources say that male life expectancy has actually dropped to as low as 55 years. Epidemics of infectious diseases run unchecked throughout the population. Bad food, lack of sewerage and sanitation, reused needles and

[51]Quoted in Kaiser, pp. 138–39.
[52]Kostikova, et al., p. 3.
[53]*Population of U.S.S.R. in 1987* (Moscow: Finansy I Statistika, 1988), p. 351.

syringes, cramped accommodations, poor personal hygiene, and poor medical care make diseases such as typhoid, hepatitis B, dysentery, and acute intestinal infections widespread in the Soviet Union. Outbreaks of cholera also occur.

Horrendous medical conditions in the Soviet Union provide the ideal base for the spread of an AIDS epidemic. The lack of disposable syringes has already had grave consequences. In January 1989, 27 children under the age of two were found infected with the AIDS virus in the rural town of Elista, deep in the heart of Russia. Hospital staff members used reusable syringes for bloodwork on 3,000 babies. Further tests on the babies found an undisclosed number of additional babies infected. One has to wonder if these tests actually served to further spread the disease, as hygienic conditions had not improved at the facility. Vadim Pokrovskiy, president of the Soviet Association in the Fight against AIDS, made the apocalyptic warning:

> Irresponsibility flourishes so much in our system that the Elista drama can be repeated in any other place. Imagine, even there, in frightened Elista, the "3-month fight against AIDS" is barely over and the sanitary epidemiological station has already registered cases of using one syringe for several patients.[54]

Rural Areas

Outside the cities, indeed, within sight of high-rise apartments on the edge of the city, life is suddenly very stark. In the Soviet Union there are no pleasant, comfortable suburbs with all the amenities of the city and huge shopping malls. Services do not extend into rural areas. Paved roads turn into mud tracks, plumbing and sewers are scarce, and electricity is unreliable. Terrible rural slums border cities and are visions of wrenching poverty and grimy neglect.

Existence is hard. Most rural-dwellers must gather wood or, if they are lucky, burn coal to heat their shacks during the long, cold winters prevalent in much of the country. Women fetch water to drink and for washing. The family clothes are sewn from available,

[54]"False Fears and the Terrible Truth; Two Competent Opinions About AIDS," Moscow *Selskaya Zhizn*, April 18, 1989, p. 4.

low-quality materials. Food is scarce in rural areas. For food, peasants have only what they can grow in small, private plots during free time from their jobs on the collective farms, plus the few livestock they are allowed to keep. Lack of feed for livestock is a serious problem, and owners resort to feeding their animals bread, which for the rural-dweller is one item that is relatively easy to obtain. Nothing is for sale in the stores, and there is not a prayer that shipments of needed goods will arrive soon. Items such as potatoes, plentiful in the cities, are scarce in the country. Unable to buy food in the stores, rural-dwellers are often reduced to stealing food from collective farms. Although peasants are the agricultural backbone of the nation, it is easier to buy food in the city than where it is actually grown. For this reason, peasants rely on Moscow shopping trips to buy food and needed consumer goods. Farmers scour the capital for deliveries and wait in line with Muscovites for the opportunity to buy goods not available where they live.

Peasants travel to railroad stations, sometimes a day's journey away, to buy black market food destined for sale in the cities. At isolated rural stops, peasants burst onto trains to buy oranges, apples, and milk from a train staff eager to pocket additional rubles for the service.

Reports from settlements all over the Soviet Union describe a severe existence unknown in the West. One Soviet journalist reports that in the Mogocha region, "Store shelves stand empty— it's a real event when they bring in three-liter jars of pickles made from over-ripe cucumbers. . . . People have to travel to the regional center for everything."[55]

Peasants have little access to common services that Americans take for granted. In the very best-served villages, there may be a seamstress from whom, after an arduous search for materials, one could get a coat or a uniform sewn. A barber might come in once a week from somewhere else, and a furniture repairman might be found. But that is the extent of services available in lucky areas. In most villages, even these minimal services are nowhere to be found.[56]

[55]Mironov, p. 3.
[56]"Portrait of a Region," *Pravda*, March 9, 1987, p. 2.

Medical care is virtually nonexistent. Villages are without even minimal health care stations. Indeed, in Pakov Province one medical worker serves dozens of small villages. This man is not even a trained doctor. He has no transportation, and locating him by telephone is difficult.[57]

Rural roads are universally bad. Road connections from collective farms to city markets are terrible. In the Komi Republic, two-thirds of the state farms are cut off from main highways. Farms have only 212 kilometers of internal roads, a tenth of what they need.[58] Dirt roads and tracks prevail in most of the countryside. Trucks carrying produce often cannot travel faster than 15 miles per hour on cratered, muddy roads.

Festering piles of rotting junk, useless products that no one wants, are a common sight in rural fields and ditches. In a discussion forum on rural problems, I. Vasiliev said, "I can't be indifferent when I see how this land has been neglected, trashed with all kinds of junk, torn up, and overgrown. I walk through the fields and my heart aches. . . . "[59] Unfortunately, unsightliness is the least of the problems. Hazardous chemicals, radioactive materials, and dangerous industrial waste are unceremoniously dumped in rural fields, without so much as a warning to the local population.

To make a bad situation worse, there is no recreation in rural areas. No forms of entertainment are available to the peasant—no movies, plays, or books. Bereft of cultural activities and stuck with the hardest lot in Soviet life, the peasant's only diversion is drink. And he drinks hard—and anything he can get his hands on. Almost everyone can buy homemade liquor or beer from neighbors who produce it on the sly. Alcoholism, rampant throughout the Soviet Union, is truly astonishing in rural areas. Collective farmers start drinking early in the morning and do not stop until they pass out, at whatever time that occurs during the day. Workers drink on the job, off the job, and during breaks from the job. They often send a coworker out for vodka runs during the day.

Rural-dwellers are isolated, and their lot is no better than that of serfs in medieval Europe. Tied to the land, they are condemned to

---

[57]V. Vorobyov and A. Murzin, "Not Just for Potatoes," *Pravda*, October 30, 1987, p. 3.

[58]"Trust Bled White," letter to the editor, *Pravda*, January 22, 1988, p. 1.

[59]Vorobyov and Murzin, p. 3.

toiling long hours for low pay with little hope of a better life. Rural workers are the lowest paid in the Soviet Union. Peasants, until recently, could not obtain internal passports to travel within the country. Now they can stay no longer than three days in a city. Still, that doesn't stop enterprising young peasants desperate to leave the land for the relatively better life of the cities. They enter military service, which gives them the right to settle in a town after their enlistment, or they marry urban residents to obtain the sought-after *propiska*, or permission, to live in a specific city or town. As a result, many villages are entirely depopulated except for a few elderly women. Decrepit shacks and tumbledown fences overgrown with weeds assault the eye in village after village.

The Soviet peasantry has borne the heaviest load under socialism. Rural workers, more than any other sector of the population, view the Communist Party as an occupying army. Village party representatives are deeply resented, because they keep peasants on the hated collective farms, do less work for more money, and live ostentatiously among peasants who cannot ever hope to live as well.

Alcoholism

Alcoholism is a national problem in the Soviet Union, which is historically a hard-drinking country. Under the Soviet government, alcoholism has reached truly staggering dimensions. Workers have few diversions and little control over their jobs, leaving them apathetic and alienated. Drink is the popular refuge for workers who want to forget the frustrations of Soviet life and drown themselves in oblivion. Losses from alcohol-related absences and drinking on the job are enormous.

In one of his early acts as general secretary, Mikhail Gorbachev limited the sales of liquor across the country. This policy has served only to anger consumers. It did not control the problem; in fact the problem became worse as workers began stealing methanol, perfumes, and alcohol-based compounds from workplaces to make deadly beverages. In 1988, New Year's programming was interrupted in Krasnodar to announce the theft of a large quantity of wood alcohol from the Krasnodar Biochemical and Vitamin Preparation Complex. The thieves were easy to find—they were staggering about in a terrible stupor and lying on the ground, poisoned by drink. At least five died and many more were taken to the hospital in serious condition.[60]

Obviously, people steal liquor from the factories that still produce it. Employees of a cognac bottler in Moscow make off with as much liquor as they can carry, while workers at a nearby beer brewery organize theft on a grand scale, setting up their own private distribution network based out of an employee's apartment. The Soviet press berates agricultural workers and vegetable transporters who steal large quantities of potatoes and grain to make bootleg liquor.

Drink-related accidents and disasters are commonplace. In one recent, dramatic instance, an experienced pilot claimed in a drunken haze that he could land his plane blindfolded. He insisted that subordinates pull down the shades of all the plane's windows and then proceeded to do just that. The pilot did manage to make a landing, but unfortunately, not at an airport. Instead, he landed smack in the middle of a town, killing 80 people.

Recognizing that limiting vodka sales has only worsened the problem while the government has lost revenues, the Soviet leadership decided to loosen the strict policy of limited sales.

Elites, Corruption, and the Black Market in the Soviet Union

While the average consumer labors to maintain a bleak existence, no longer looking forward to a distant future of abundance, Soviet elites have enjoyed an economy that works well only for them. The top echelon of Soviet society, formed by party political administrators known as the *nomenklatura*, has lived extremely well by any Russian standard. Lenin himself was responsible for creating this elite class, which he called the "revolutionary vanguard" of the Communist Party.

Under communism, state ownership of the means of production was supposed to bring about the workers' ownership of everything, but in fact the bureaucratic class became the owner of national property, as Milovan Djilas, former member of the Yugoslavian Politburo, explained in his classic book *The New Class:*

> Property is legally considered social and national property. But in actuality, a single group manages it in its own interest.
> . . . The new class instinctively feels that national goods are,

[60]K. Aksyonov, "They Wanted to Drink," *Pravda*, January 10, 1988, p. 3.

in fact, its property, and that even the terms "socialist,"
"social," and "state" property denote a general legal fiction.
. . . The discrepancy between legal and actual conditions
continually results in obscure and abnormal social and economic relationships. It also means that the words of the
leading group do not correspond to its actions; and that all
actions result in strengthening its property holdings and its
political position.[61]

Stalin greatly expanded the Soviet bureaucracy to oversee the
mass collectivization programs, the huge industrial projects, and
the purges. To attract young communists, Stalin announced that
equality was dead and only "worthy of a primitive sect of ascetics
but not of a socialist society organized on Marxist lines."[62] From
then on, it was every communist for himself.

Party members walled themselves off from the hardships
wrought by their own policies. They created a closed society whose
members enjoy all manner of privileges, perks, and status symbols
far from the prying eyes of the masses. They surrounded themselves with special stores, special medical care, exclusive resorts,
and country houses. They ensured the best education for their
children and reserved the best jobs for themselves.

By the beginning of 1990, Gorbachev's policy of glasnost had led
to such criticism of the system of privileges that the Politburo was
forced to curtail them, its own included. How uniformly throughout
the country this ruling will be implemented and the extent to which
the privileges will be reduced in practice remain to be seen. If
Gorbachev continues to succeed in shifting political power away
from the Communist Party, its privileges, like those of aristocrats,
will disappear.

In the midst of poverty, the leaders justified their plenty as com-
pensation for services rendered to the workers. The hapless worker,
of course, would be hard put to say just what these services are.
As Djilas acknowledges:

He who grabs power grabs privileges and indirectly grabs
property. Consequently, in Communism, power or politics

[61]Milovan Djilas, *The New Class—An Analysis of the Communist System* (New York:
Praeger, 1957), p. 65.

[62]Josef Stalin, *Problems of Leninism*, authorized English translation from 11th Russian ed. (Moscow, 1945), p. 502.

as a profession is the ideal of those who have the desire or
the prospect of living as parasites at the expense of others.[63]

One's position within the elite determines the standard of living
obtainable. At the very pinnacle, a group of about two dozen of the
top leaders and their families live off the fat of the land. Gorbachev
and company are chauffeured about in specially manufactured Zil
limousines, while the average citizen, who does not even own a
car, looks on as the luxury vehicles speed by with police escorts.
The privileges of the elite include country houses or *dachas*, with
servants, swimming pools, and the finest caviar and vodka. Armed
men guard hidden entrances to these palaces to prevent the curious
from gaining a glimpse of the extravagance. And far be it from the
leaders to stand in lines like mere mortals. Instead, they pay a
nominal fee to the sumptuous Kremlin canteen to get the very best
caviar, meats, fish, vegetables, and fruits delivered to their homes.
Wives of the elite are entitled to maids to do the cooking and
cleaning. Personal needs—barbers, tailors, the finest medical
care—are all part of the package. All in all, a Politburo member
enjoys a singularly idyllic existence, which is comparable to life for
the ruling family under the tsars.

Below the top leadership are other privileged officials holding
prestigious jobs in the Central Committee of the party, in the
regional party offices, in the ministerial bureaucracy, in factories, in
the propaganda machine, and in the diplomatic corps. An estimated
three million people in the country belong to this elite class. Every
rank in the hierarchy is imbued with corresponding privileges.
Officials at each rung can see the perks that the next level will bring,
and they curry favor to win promotions. A deputy minister eats in
a different dining room with better-quality food than a mid-level
functionary in the same ministry. In turn, middle managers eat
vastly superior food in their dining room compared to the food
available in the dining room reserved for clerks and other low-level
personnel. This system of privileges is based on discrimination that
permeates the entire country.

Mid-level bureaucrats in the Central Committee are entitled to 30
days of vacation a year, plus travel time, a benefit that U.S. execu-
tives would consider quite generous. Better yet, they pay almost

[63]Djilas, p. 46.

nothing for a relaxing vacation at an exclusive Central Committee rest home, where they enjoy luxury accommodations and leisure activities such as tennis and boating. Even if these bureaucrats decide to take their vacation at a remote resort, they would find that the town party committee had a dacha available for nomenklatura members. Depending upon their rank within the hierarchy, officials have been entitled to the use of a dacha, a piece of land on which to build a dacha (using stolen state materials), or, for very high-level officials, the land and the dacha itself.

In addition, officials have been entitled to coupons allowing them to purchase various amounts of quality foods at the Kremlin canteen. The higher the officials, the better the special store they can enter and the less they pay for higher-quality food and consumer goods. The stores stock scarce imported items and foods along with the best Soviet production. Ordinary citizens cannot enter the special stores and even if they could, the stores do not accept regular rubles.

Officials have routinely diverted state funds and resources to their own personal uses. State budgets provide a never-ending source of goodies, permitting officials to allocate gifts—cars, imported furniture, and other luxury goods—to themselves. Pilfering the best wood, bricks, and other building materials to construct their dachas, they call skilled plumbers, electricians, and construction workers away from their regular jobs. Construction and repair of the elite's work places are done immediately, without the usual interminable waiting period.

Members of the nomenklatura need not fear for their children's prospects. Young members of this group are well cared for. At the tender age of five there is already competition among the youngsters over who comes to kindergarten in the best car and who has the best toys. By the time the youngster is ready to attend college, parental connections ensure entrance to the best university. Daddy's contacts are enough to ensure that the privileged youth passes the entrance exams, even if said youth never opened a book before that date. To cover living expenses, these students receive stipends from the state that are not much lower than their teachers' salaries. Upon graduation from an elite university, the young nomenklaturist knows a limitless future. The best jobs are offered on a silver platter. In sum, the offspring of the privileged are coddled and cosseted from the very beginning; they never know the hardships of ordinary Soviet life.

Resentment runs high among the populace. People are tired of the never-ending struggle to provision themselves and are aware of the contents of the nondescript, nameless buildings that house elite stores, luxury apartments, and exclusive restaurants. Workers fume about the hypocrisy of a society that is called classless by the rulers but that in reality consists of widely divergent classes: rulers who have everything and workers who have nothing.

To join this aristocracy, one must first have a party card. Ambitious outsiders have focused on joining the party at all costs, even taking low-level jobs in provincial bureaucracies. To join, an outsider must get in the good graces of party officials and prevail on them to recommend him or her for membership. The privileges available for rank-and-file party functionaries are few, but a cushy life awaits those who are obsequious to their superiors and avoid rocking the boat. Managers promote subordinates who show a gift for flattery and for avoiding responsibility. Merit is rarely a factor in promotion decisions and, in fact, can impede a functionary's prospects. In this system, mediocrity rises to the top as underqualified superiors promote similar subordinates. Political activism, social contacts, and total conformity pave the way for success in the Soviet Union.

Typically, ambitious regional party secretaries think of themselves as masters of all they survey and use their power to create their own personal fiefdoms. They treat their subordinates like dirt, while fawning over superiors. As long as they retain the favor of their superiors, they have a large measure of independence and are able to rule people under their domain.

Members of the elite have had to pay for their position in society, however. More than anyone else, they have had to adhere strictly to the party line and rapidly accommodate to shifts in order to avoid losing their privileges. A command to perpetrate corruption must be obeyed. No voice of conscience can intervene, or all could be lost. Everyone owes his position to the good graces of several other people who can withdraw their favor at any time.

While the Soviet elites live sumptuously compared to the ordinary masses, the quality of the goods they consume is no better than what the working class of the United States can obtain. In 1989 the Central Committee's hotel in Moscow, which was luxuriously appointed with chandeliers and spacious suites the size of large apartments, was provisioned with harsh, brown pumice-like bars of bath soap and with toilet paper made from thin sheets of slick paper. The food at the elite hotel restaurant could not be described as appetizing to the Western palate, and it would face stiff competition from U.S. coach-class airline food.

The Soviet Union is handicapped by a parasitic group that is slowly draining the life from the economy. Unfettered by moral restraint and legal codes, important members of the ruling class extract resources from the economy in the manner of feudal barons. Corruption, inevitable whenever one group enjoys such control over resources, abounds in the Soviet Union.

In a famous case, Vasily Mzhavanadze, Politburo member from the Soviet republic of Georgia, was in cahoots with Otari Laziashvili, the Soviet version of the mafia godfather, in the operation of a large network of underground factories and retail outlets near Tbilisi. The factories, using stolen state resources and production time, produced all kinds of consumer goods such as sweaters, scarves, plastic raincoats, and nylon mesh shopping bags. The items were sold on the black market.

Laziashvili became an underground multimillionnaire, and through his contacts with Mzhavanadze he was able to hire and fire at will high party officials in the city of Tbilisi and even in the republic of Georgia. There was a brisk trade in ministerial posts in the republic, with lucrative positions in the Ministry of Trade or the Ministry of Light Industry fetching up to 300,000 rubles. Practically everyone in the region knew about the activity. Finally, it attracted too much attention. Laziashvili, along with 82 accomplices, was indicted for robbing the state of 1.7 million rubles. In actuality, the sum was much higher than that, for his empire covered the entire Georgian republic. But Kremlin officials hushed up the scandal around Mzhavanadze, who was not prosecuted. He did have to step down in 1972, but not before he too had become a multimillionnaire. What was unusual about the case was that Mzhavanadze and his accomplices were not allowed to continue indefinitely. Instead he was dumped from the Politburo. While the scale of his corruption exceeded the bounds of the acceptable, shady activities are commonplace.[64]

Another web of corruption led to the 1988 conviction of Yuri Churbanov, the son-in-law of Brezhnev, for accepting more than $1 million in bribes while working for the Interior Ministry in the Uzbekistan Republic. Although he was the most famous of the accused, Churbanov was part of a vast gangster network that was plaguing the entire republic and was run by Sharaf Rashidov, Communist Party secretary of Uzbekistan. A Western journalist reports that the republic "was a swamp of corruption, with Rashidov filling every post of consequence with his cronies and handing out state awards, such as the Order of Lenin, not for merit but for bribes of hundreds of thousands of rubles."[65] The Uzbek mafia chiefs ran the state cotton industry, the major industry of the republic, for their own enrichment. They built palatial summer homes for themselves, dressed in high style in furs and jewels, ate the finest foods, and drank imported liquors. This mob ran the republic with an iron fist and with a penchant for hiring professional killers when someone refused to cooperate.[66] Mikhail Gorbachev seems determined to stamp out such activity, and investigations are under way.

In another incident, high-ranking party members were caught smuggling caviar out of the country in large tins marked pickled herring. The purchasers were making hard currency payments into the Soviet officials' Swiss bank accounts.

Selling scarce consumer goods on the black market figures prominently in Soviet corruption scandals. Ordinary consumers, who can not find any goods in the state stores, will pay premium prices in the black market for stolen state goods. Officials take advantage of consumers' desperation (caused by the officials' own policies) to collect huge sums in bribes, kickbacks, and black market sales.

[64]Konstantin Simis, *USSR: The Corrupt Society,* translated by Jacqueline Edwards and Mitchell Schneider (New York: Simon and Schuster, 1982), pp. 53–60. Also see Hedrick Smith, *The Russians,* revised ed. (New York: Ballantine Books, 1976), pp. 128–29.

[65]David Remnick, "Corrupt Soviet Uzbekistan Learns About 'Our Rotten History,'" *Washington Post,* October 7, 1988, p. A1.

[66]Vladimir Sokolov, "Gang Rule," *Literaturnaya Gazeta,* August 17, 1988, p. 13; also see Remnick.

Ordinary people, no less than higher-ups, also set themselves up to profit from any special advantage they may have in their jobs. For example, Irina, a salesclerk in a meat store, knows the delivery schedule for meats to the store. She sells that information to eager consumers for one ruble, and for another ruble she will reserve a half-way decent piece of meat for a customer. She steals as much as she can of each delivery of meat, and she resells it to acquaintances on the black market at many times the state-set price. Sometimes she barters stolen meat for a new dress made by an expert seamstress who steals materials from the textile factory where she works. Or she may exchange her knowledge of meat deliveries for a tip about upcoming deliveries of lettuce to the grocer. There are any number of ways that Irina profits from her low-paid position in the meat store.

The focus of the new in-depth reporting of corruption in the Soviet press is beginning to shift from outlying republics to Moscow. Continual diatribes against corruption in the Communist Party suggest that an extreme level of corruption pervades the entire economic system.

As one result of pervasive corruption, Moscow has effectively lost control over the rest of the country. Republic-level officials, colluding in corrupt activities, can easily conspire to ignore the latest decree from Moscow. Provincial officials have become akin to feudal lords, using their independent power bases to jockey for position and territory.

4. The Original Aspirations and the Soviet Economy Today

The Soviets live under such an irrational system because they took Marx seriously. They were intent on establishing a radically different form of economic organization that would be more productive than and morally superior to a market economy and that would provide the basis for a new society.

To understand the working of the Soviet economy today, we must examine Marx's theories. Marx believed that the institutions and consciousness of people in each historical period are determined by the economic organization of society. This view is known as the doctrine of "historical materialism," which Marx expressed as follows:

> The mode of production of material life conditions the general process of social, political, and intellectual life. It is not the consciousness of men that determines their existence, but their social existence that determines their consciousness.[1]

By this statement, Marx meant that a feudal economy begat a feudal consciousness and corresponding political systems and values. The feudal economy evolved into a capitalist economy and wrought a bourgeois or capitalist political superstructure resting on the new economic foundation. A feudal economy cannot generate a capitalist consciousness—only a market system can. In turn, only a socialist economy can generate a socialist consciousness, the necessary basis for a socialist government.

Marx believed that the capitalist economy is destined to go through crisis after crisis—cycles of inflation and unemployment—until it collapses from its internal contradiction, which stems from

---

[1]Karl Marx, *A Contribution to the Critique of Political Economy* (New York: International Publishers, 1970), pp. 20–21.

separating production from use. A socialist economy would then emerge just as capitalism emerged from feudalism; new institutions and values—a whole new way of life—would develop, making possible a socialist government.

Marx believed that capitalism was destined for failure because its commodity mode of production separates production from use. According to him, production for sale or exchange in the market always results in overproduction and the "anarchy of the market." Each firm plans its own production, but from the standpoint of society as a whole, production is unplanned. The capitalist cannot predict the price at which consumers will buy, whom consumers will be, or even whether they will buy at all. All of these things remain to be determined in the market. Consequently, human beings are pushed around by market forces—the forces of their own making. Instead of ruling their own activities, people are ruled by them and live an alienated existence.[2]

Marx rejected market society as an unscientific way of life. He believed that production should be planned for direct use and distributed in kind, thus eliminating market exchange and the crises and alienation that result from it. Centrally planned production for direct use by society emerged as the definition of scientific socialism.

Marx never supplied the specifics of how socialism or communism would work out the plan that replaces market organization. He did say the planned economy would have no commodity production, no market exchange among individual producers or between producers and consumers, no money, no private property, no economic crises, and no alienation. Central economic planning for direct use was to organize all of society into one huge extended family, with rural workers producing agricultural products for distribution to the towns and industrial workers producing goods for distribution to the farms.

The readiness of 19th- and early 20th-century intellectuals to swallow this theory can, in part, be explained by the times. Countless innovations in the sciences led to improvements in the well-being of man. The invention of the steam engine, for instance,

[2]See Paul Craig Roberts and Matthew A. Stephenson, *Marx's Theory of Exchange, Alienation, and Crisis* (Stanford, Calif.: Hoover Institution Press, 1973).

precipitated the development of numerous labor-saving devices. Medical advances lowered mortality rates and helped people to live longer, healthier lives than ever before. Superstitions and traditions relating to all aspects of life were daily being discarded. Social thinkers observed developments in the sciences and reasoned that the social organization of society could also be improved once privilege and tradition were swept away. At the same time, business cycles were associated with a new social ill of widespread unemployment. In place of the overworked serf were dispossessed and unemployed workers forced to sell their labor for whatever it would bring in the market. Many social thinkers were disturbed that the market rewarded people in ways contrary to social justice, as dramatized by Charles Dickens in his famous Christmas story. Intellectuals believed that it was possible to develop a superior society on the basis of scientific principles. Many eagerly awaited the advent of someone to point the way toward the use of science in remaking society.

Although Marx provided no blueprint for implementing his radical ideas, his idea of purposefully planning production rather than allowing it to occur haphazardly, as under capitalism, sounded scientific to his followers. He also found ready supporters among people who craved power and saw his theory as a justification for sweeping away the old order.

In 1917, Vladimir Lenin and his ragged band of Bolsheviks, a Marxist faction, seized power in Russia in the name of a socialist revolution. This action shocked orthodox Marxists because it flouted the doctrine of historical materialism. Russia did not even have a capitalist economy; it was still in the last throes of feudalism. Yet Lenin was proclaiming a socialist government. Intense criticism focused on the upstart Lenin, and he was isolated from most Marxist believers and attacked for his deviations.

Lenin was in a quandary. The Marxists' criticism stung him to the core. But he wanted to act and not wait for history. Writing in September 1917 in "The Impending Catastrophe and How to Combat It," Lenin said that one cannot be a revolutionary if one fears to advance toward socialism. He characterized the other Russian Marxists, the Social Revolutionaries and the Mensheviks, as "pseudo-Marxist lackeys of the bourgeoisie" for claiming that it is too

77

early to establish socialism in Russia.[3] He asserted that the need for central control of the economy "is indisputable and universally recognized."[4]

The path was clear: Lenin immediately embarked on a transition to a socialist economy in order to provide the necessary basis for his socialist government. A series of measures that later became known as "war communism" were quickly implemented to transform the Russian economy into a socialist one.[5] He nationalized the banks and factories and set up an administrative apparatus to exchange the products of the town for the products of the countryside. The nationalizations so disorganized production, however, that output levels plummeted and there was nothing to distribute to the peasants in return for their products. The policy degenerated to outright confiscation in which foodstuffs were seized from peasants.

The extent of the Bolsheviks' faith in Marxism and the seriousness of their attempt to establish a socialist, centrally planned economy in Russia cannot be overemphasized. They profoundly believed that they were Marxist visionaries who would make the Russian economy the envy of the world. At the same time, the heady power they wielded fed their utopian aspirations, pressing them to redouble their efforts to impose a program that was meeting with widespread resistance within the country.

By 1921 the country was in a shambles. Peasant rebellions were commonplace, and the factory workers who were supposed to be the backbone of the revolution chimed in and demanded an end to the chaos. Factory strikes took place even in Petrograd, a communist stronghold, and were commonplace in the industrial region of the Urals and in Izhevsk where an army of 30,000 men was formed that eventually fought against the revolution. With their close ties to the land still intact, industrial workers began flowing back to rural areas on a large scale. The Armenians rose and captured the regional capital of Yerevan in February 1921. In West Siberia almost 60,000 peasants mobilized an uprising in January 1921 that spread over 12 districts, and they captured a number of important towns.

[3]V. I. Lenin, *Collected Works,* English translation, Vol. 25, (London: Lawrence & Wishart, 1960–1968), pp. 356–57.

[4]Lenin, p. 324.

[5]See Paul Craig Roberts, *Alienation and the Soviet Economy* (Albuquerque: University of New Mexico Press, 1971).

Finally, the critical moment was reached in March when the sailors at the Kronstadt Naval Base rebelled and turned Soviet guns on the Soviet government itself.

The widespread political and economic opposition to the Bolsheviks was one of fundamental principle. As George Katkov wrote, it had finally dawned on the populace what the Bolsheviks' ideal society meant:

> All efforts of individual members of the community were to be regimented so as to serve exclusively the needs of society as a whole. What these needs were was to be determined by the Communist leadership of the State, which undertook, in exchange for their loyalty and total submission to the State and Party directives, to provide for all individual citizens those needs which the leadership considered legitimate. This Marxist ideal was fundamentally unacceptable not only to the peasantry, but also to a large part of the town proletariat.[6]

Lenin came to realize that his attempt to stamp out commodity production and to establish socialist planning was a serious threat to the political survival of the Bolsheviks. This threat loomed larger and larger until it displaced in Lenin's mind the threat posed by failure to meet the requirements of historical materialism and to construct a socialist economy as the basis for a socialist government.

By March 1921 the massive unrest convinced Lenin to settle for temporarily abandoning the attempt to socialize the economy. Until Gorbachev's perestroika, Lenin's move was the only real retreat from the Marx-inspired system of central planning in Soviet history. The Bolsheviks proclaimed the "New Economic Policy" and allowed markets to revive. Lenin still believed, however, that commodity production posed a threat to the political survival of the Bolsheviks. A man of lesser conviction would have been unable to reconcile Marxist theory with an intractable reality, but Lenin stayed true to dogma by rationalizing that, despite commodity production, the socialist political "superstructure" could be maintained for an indeterminate but finite period by party control of the "commanding heights."

---

[6]George Katkov, "The Kronstadt Rising," *St. Antony's Papers*, no. 6 (London: Chatto & Windus, 1959), p. 51.

Lenin sought to use his New Economic Policy to consolidate power by increasing production, an action that he claimed would also give the Bolsheviks time to instill a socialist consciousness in the populace. With output and consciousness at higher levels, he believed a second attempt to achieve socialist economic organization would be successful. Following Lenin's death in 1924, implementation of central planning remained a necessary ingredient for the survival of a socialist government in Russia.[7]

After he consolidated power, Stalin began where Lenin left affairs. Eager to renew efforts to socialize the economy, in early 1928 Stalin introduced emergency measures to confiscate grain from the peasants. The market-based New Economic Policy came to an end, along with the incentives to produce that it had restored.

Stalin relentlessly pursued an assault on private property to create the system of central planning envisioned by Marx. Stalin lessened pressure for socialization only at times when he had no choice, regrouping forces to renew efforts later in a burst of fervor. Perhaps recalling the years of war communism, Stalin said that direct exchange between town and country would have

> to be introduced without any particular hurry and only as the products of the town multiply. But it must be introduced unswervingly and unhesitatingly, step by step contracting the sphere of operation of commodity circulation and widening the sphere of operations of products-exchange.
>
> Such a system, by contracting the sphere of operation of commodity circulation, will facilitate the transition from socialism to communism. Moreover, it will make it possible to include the basic property of the collective farms, the product of collective farming, in the general system of national planning.[8]

The brutal collectivization and ensuing famine, the slave labor camps, and the purges of the Communist Party were consequences of a fanatic adherence to ideology. The bureaucracy originated by Lenin ballooned under the demand for administrators—someone had to oversee the efforts to transform the economy.

[7]See Roberts, pp. 35–40.

[8]Josef Stalin, *Economic Problems of Socialism in the USSR* (New York: International Publishers, 1952), p. 70.

After crushing the peasants with the collectivization and famine of the early 1930s, Stalin was still not pleased with the results of his handiwork. Market relations existed between the collectivized farms and the state, which paid the farms for their output and sold food in the stores for money. Stalin saw the problem, as Lenin had before him, as one of not enough industrial products to distribute to farmers in exchange for their foodstuffs.

Stalin concentrated efforts on a crash industrialization program. The first Five-Year Plan had been approved in 1929. With targets denominated in gross output, the plan recognized only the faintest relationship between actual resources and production possibilities. Instead, it was "merely a body of figures which were constantly being scaled upward."[9] Every succeeding plan prescribed higher, more ambitious, and more impossible targets to reach than the last. Stalin applied terror to get the country to work to a frenzy meeting illogical, poorly conceived gross output quotas.

Assuming that bigger is always better, Stalin built mammoth industrial complexes, which drew heavily on the vast supplies of slave labor created by the police apparatus. Little thought was given to the efficiency or even feasibility of such plants. In fact, planners went out of their way to locate them in barren areas devoid of electricity, gas lines, and railroads. All too often even the land was unsuitable. Stalin, a bookkeeper by training, lacked experience in economic affairs. Management and workers who did not meet work norms often ended up in labor camps.

This massive industrialization effort did not bring about the abundance of products needed to abolish the market. Undeterred, Stalin insisted that

> collective-farm output must be excluded from the system of commodity circulation and included in the system of products-exchange between state industry and the collective farms.[10]

Reality, however, refused to accept this ideological system, and the Bolsheviks never succeeded in their efforts to remake the Soviet economy into a centrally directed administrative system of products

[9]Moshe Lewin, *Political Undercurrents in Soviet Economic Debates* (Princeton: Princeton University Press, 1974), p. 453.

[10]Stalin, p. 70.

exchange. They were unable to do away with money. Money relations exist throughout the economy, and the centralized supply distribution system, cornerstone of their efforts, is a notorious failure. They did succeed in suppressing rationality, however, by abolishing price and profit signals and the incentive of private property. The result is a system that is more or less organized like a market but without the rational criteria of markets.

In the Soviet Union there is no central planning in a Marxian or even in a Western sense. The famous central plan is essentially a summation of the individual plans originating in the enterprises. In effect, the average firm's plan or target has been set in the following way. Managers are asked how much they can produce and the inputs they require. To gain leeway and a safety factor to ensure their success, managers misrepresent figures on both counts. They understate their productive capacity and overstate their resource requirements. Planners understand the game and know that managers misrepresent, but if managers have been careful in the past and have never significantly overproduced their target, they will win the game and get a target that is safely within the productive capabilities of their factories. Managers want targets or quotas that they can easily make because their income is maximized by making and slightly exceeding a quota. If they greatly exceed it, they give themselves away and risk a target in the future that strains or exceeds their productive capacity.

If we look at this managerial behavior in organizational terms, we find that it gives the Soviet manager an autonomous role that is inconsistent with a hierarchic, planned economy. Soviet managers may have more formal restraints than their Western counterparts, but, like Western managers, they are essentially autonomous in that they organize production by maximizing their own benefits. The difference between the Soviet and the Western manager lies essentially in the signals that they interpret. Western managers organize production by interpreting price and profit movements, whereas Soviet managers have interpreted "success indicators" (which have essentially revolved around the gross output indicator).[11] This difference is very real in terms of consumer satisfaction,

[11]See Roberts; also see E. G. Dolan, "An Experimental Polycentric Model of the Soviet Economy," in Judith Thornton (ed.), *Economic Analysis of the Soviet-Type System* (Cambridge: Cambridge University Press, 1976), pp. 125–40.

but it is not an organizational difference. It has allowed Soviet managers to be successful even though their output is poorly related to users' needs. In this, Soviet managers have enjoyed a freedom not known to their Western counterparts.

Western observers have been aware of the behavior of Soviet managers for many years, but they failed to realize its organizational meaning. They were misled by numerous detailed instructions that seem to completely circumscribe Soviet managers' decisions, leaving no room for maneuver in the way they carry out their assigned tasks, much less allowing them control over their output assortment. The detailed instructions made it look as if the Soviet manager was a mere cog in a vast hierarchy. If one looks from inside the system, however, the myriad instructions or orders from the planning authorities have the paradoxical effect of freeing the manager from central control. For example, the Hungarian economist, Tibor Liska, has written:

> As the number of directives to be observed increases, the more detailed and the stricter they become in a most intricate economic life hardly lending itself to standardization, the greater the liberty of individual planners and economic managers. The intricacy of economic life follows, namely, primarily from the fact that hosts of contrary tendencies must be brought into harmony with optimum efficiency. The stricter and more rigid the regulations prescribing the enforcement of such contrary tendencies, the more contradictory the directives must become. One receiving the directives has but a single choice: *not to observe all the directives.* On the other hand, in the decision to keep to one out of the necessarily contradictory directives, and drop the others, as well as in aiming at the issue of certain directives, he has a freedom almost greater than the most sovereign of tyrants.[12]

[12]Tibor Liska, "The Development of Market Relations and of the Theory and Practice of Price Mechanism in Socialism," lecture given at CESES International Seminar on Problems of Planning in Eastern Europe, Tremezzo, Italy, July 1967, mimeographed, p. 4. The de facto economic autonomy of managers is extra legal and does not translate into political power or political freedom. Indeed, since Soviet managers can function only by committing crimes against the state, their awareness that they can be prosecuted at any time for economic crimes has restrained their participation in political protest.

Not even the supply system is centrally planned. It is well known that the general supply system contains real market elements. Black markets are extensive and essential to the functioning of the economy. But even the official or "centrally planned" supply apparatus functions organizationally like a market.[13] This function becomes clear once we focus on the managers' procurement activities, that is, on their exertion of pressure on central planners who, in effect, are turned into supply agents for the managers.

Despite the plan's intent, managers of Soviet firms act to maximize their own benefits, not the society's or the planning board's or the party's. These managers have cost and benefit functions, and they weigh the costs of exerting procurement pressure against the benefits of making and slightly exceeding their targets. In their cost function are such things as the money and purchase authorizations used through official channels; the cost of using a limited budget of credibility, good will, influence, and connections; the psychological cost of battling red tape; the cost of black market purchases and of hiring a procurement staff (expediters); and the risk of criminal prosecution. Benefits are the usual ones of monetary reward, promotion, and fame.

In this system the planner really heads a central inventory, controls the rate of shipment of a given product or input from the inventory, and divides the shipment among competing users. Among the many factors that affect the planner's decisions are the quantity available for shipment, the backlog of unfilled orders, the amount of procurement pressure exerted by any firm's manager for the fulfillment of given orders, and the priority rating of the user. There is substitution between the last two factors. The lower the priority rating of each manager, the greater must be that manager's exertion of procurement pressure. As managers' priority ratings rise, the procurement pressure that they must exert lessens.

Obviously, if managers' supplies of inputs always arrive on time and in the correct amounts, they enjoy a system that maximizes their own benefits. But the average manager must compete for inputs through every available channel.

The system has feedbacks that carry information on scarcities. Inventory build-ups indicate inputs that are produced in excess

[13]See Roberts; see also Dolan.

relative to demands, whereas the greater the demand for an input, the higher the procurement cost. When the deliveries of an input get seriously behind the demands for it, the planner responds to the increasing pressure exerted by managers and reassigns priorities, thus turning the lagging sector into a priority sector. Assigning a higher priority to a sector subsidizes its procurement efforts, thus decreasing its costs and raising the level of output that maximizes the manager's welfare. Simulations of this process have shown that if the procurement pressure mechanism is stopped from operating and if managers are forced to abide by the formal rules, the economic system collapses. And indeed it would. Failures of the official supply system are notorious. They are acknowledged by the Soviet state through its toleration of extensive and illegal black market activities.

It is clear that planning in the Soviet Union has not involved deriving the structure of output for the economy as a whole, much less an optimal structure. Instead, the efforts of the planning apparatus have gone into the central supply system. In practice this system functions as a supply agent for the enterprises and tries to ensure that enterprises get resources consistent with their productive capabilities. As many Soviet writers have pointed out, all the irrationalities of the planning system could be abolished by simply requiring that factories produce to meet customers' orders and judging their success in terms of profitability.

Over the years, the impossibility of achieving a noncommodity form of production in a complex economy has produced sufficient frustration and economic irrationality to weaken and undermine the ideological program for the economy. Today the system of material supply—the backbone of the administered economy—is an institutional legacy of forgotten or vaguely understood aspirations. In the ruins of the ideological program to transform man by transforming the economy lives a bureaucratic vested interest. Will Soviet leaders be able to overcome powerful vested interests and lead their country into capitalism?

5. Is the Soviet System Redeemable?

When Gorbachev began his political and economic reforms, many raised the question, Is communism reversible? But this question assumed that communism was achieved. Instead, it failed, and the real question is, How long can failure be sustained? Not much longer, it would seem. How else can one explain the rise of Gorbachev and the fact that the Communist Party itself made him general secretary?

Many people in the Soviet Union understand that planning does not work. In our conversations with Gorbachev's advisers, it is clear that they understand that profitability must replace the gross output indicator as the signal of managerial success and that private property must be established if the Soviet economy is to benefit from market incentives.

Soviet economists are no longer hesitant to express these views publicly and forcefully. For example, Vasili Selyunin wrote in *Komsomolskaya Pravda* on January 17, 1990, that

> directive planning is the core of the command economy. Whether you tighten it up or not, the result is well known: Plans have nothing to do with real life. . . . We know what changes are necessary and what order they should be carried out in. Prices will have to be freed; we will have to stop paying workers who produce goods the market does not want.[1]

In *Sotsialisticheskaya Industriya* on December 12, 1989, Yaroslav Kuzminov said that "the experience gained in world economics proves very well that state ownership and ownership by the state are

---

[1]Vasili Selyunin, "As Bad as It's Going to Get?" Moscow *Komsomolskaya Pravda*, January 17, 1990, p. 1.

inefficient and burdensome forms of economic activity for the society."[2] The Marxian goal of replacing commodity production with central economic planning seems absurd to modern Soviet economists who, instead, attribute the problems of the Soviet economy to the absence of commodity production:

> Essentially, we are not a commodity production system, and it is for this reason that we do not have the elements of a developed market economy: A market of commodities, manpower, and capital. Accordingly, our money is not real; it is semi-money and semi-coupons for the purposeful acquisition of what is necessary, and, more accurately, what is allowed.[3]

Stanislav S. Shatalin, a member of Gorbachev's Presidential Council, warned in *Pravda* that if economic change does not take place, "We will find ourselves in a common grave. While private ownership has already proved socially useful throughout the world, our state ownership has only proved that it can land the country in a mess."[4]

According to Gorbachev, "If we do not get out of the system we're in—excuse my rough talk—then everything living in our society will die."[5]

However, without a broader context of change, even thoroughgoing economic reforms would probably fail. The problem is that decades of an administered economy and political unaccountability have encrusted the Soviet Union with vested interests and "back channel" operations that simply make the whole system unresponsive to the General Secretary. Once Gorbachev realized that this formerly powerful position had short arms, he began shaking up the system in search of new levers of power. Without this power, he cannot overcome the vested interests that oppose his economic

[2]Ye. Leontyeva, report on interview with Yaroslav Kuzminov, senior scientific associate at the USSR Academy of Sciences Institute of Economics, "We Discuss the Draft Law on Ownership: To Strengthen Stability Against Misfortune?" Moscow *Sotsialisticheskaya Industriya*, December 12, 1989, p. 2.

[3]Soltan Dzarasov, "Reform: Reality and Prospects," Moscow *Sotsialisticheskaya Industriya*, November 11, 1989, p. 2.

[4]Francis X. Clines, "Gorbachev Urges New Economy," *New York Times*, April 27, 1990, p. A6.

[5]Ibid.

reforms. Without an economic transformation, the Soviet Union is a spent force in history.

This general realization is why the Communist Party supported Gorbachev's efforts despite the threat to its perks, status, and power. Discontent to preside over decline, Gorbachev and his supporters are attempting to create a popular base for centralized power by resurrecting long-suppressed institutions of religion, private property, and the ballot box. He is betting that if he relieves people of tyrannies and gives them economic opportunities and a voice, they will support him. If his confidence in the people is justified, Gorbachev will win, and the Soviet Union will be transformed.

There is a tendency among some to see the reformers as entirely motivated by goodwill and their opponents by vested interests. Gorbachev is bringing goodwill back into Soviet political life, but there is as much self-interest in the reform effort as there is among its opponents. Gorbachev's supporters understand that the slippage of the Soviet economy is a threat to the country's power and influence. His opponents are content with their positions as petty tyrants and feudal nobles. Not all kings in efforts to recentralize power won their struggles with the barons, who preferred it the way they had it; that is why Gorbachev is attempting to mobilize the people.

It is a risky game. For Gorbachev's economic reforms to succeed, he must terminate the gross output indicator and socialized (state) property. This change directly threatens massive vested interests and is a revolutionary move in itself. Since his reforms can be easily resisted by those they undercut, he is forced to create new political mechanisms in order to recentralize power and gain leverage. This is also a revolutionary step, and its consequences are as unpredictable as those that followed from Louis XVI calling the Estates-General.

Gorbachev might become a popular leader and occupy a governing role equivalent in power to a constitutional monarch. The task he faces is immense, but there have been some in history whose accomplishments earned them the appellation "the great."

Whether Gorbachev succeeds or fails, change is under way. And change means uncertainty and instability as the struggle is waged. In the West, bedeviled by problems that are minor in the Soviet scheme of things and accustomed to leaders who can hardly walk and chew gum at the same time, there is little comprehension of the enormity of the task Gorbachev faces or of the extraordinary courage and determination Gorbachev has displayed by undertaking the task.

Arrayed against Gorbachev is a network of regional and local party secretaries, top factory bureaucrats, and ministry officials— people who wield extraordinary power and devote their energies to personal gain. Rapacious officials do as they please because they are secure in their fiefdoms; are in control of state resources; and are bolstered by blackmail, brutality, and manipulation. And because they do not have to be accountable, they are absolute rulers of their territories. The purpose of Gorbachev's glasnost (openness) is to expose and topple them with publicity campaigns. Articles decrying feudalism now appear regularly in the Soviet press, and this element of the ruling class is now routinely described as gangsters, mobsters, and khans.[6] Even these terms downplay their power as these rulers are not confined to the underworld or black market but control every kind of legitimate state activity. To the dismay of reformers, an army of robber barons, unfettered by law, largely runs the country.

With many restraints on the Soviet press removed by glasnost, a picture of Soviet reality has emerged that strains the Western imagination. On January 20, 1988, the news magazine *Literaturnaya Gazeta* reported the case of Akhmadzhan Adylov, director of the Pap Agro-Industrial Production Association, a huge complex that covers an entire region in Uzbekistan and is the size of a medieval barony.

Adylov was decorated with the Soviet Union's highest awards while he carved out a vast territory for his personal fiefdom, complete with dungeons for uncooperative inhabitants. As the magazine reported, Adylov

> crushed all the authorities in the district and province. Police personnel received assignments from him, and if the orders were not carried out, he could have them beaten up or

[6]Vladimir Sokolov, "Gang Rule," *Literaturnaya Gazeta*, August 17, 1988, p. 13; also A. Uglanov, "Not Only Punishment," *Argumenty i Fakty*, September 3–9, 1988, pp. 6–7.

dismissed from their jobs. And who were the police, anyway, to someone who had dumped a province Party secretary who didn't suit him and openly threatened his successor with reprisals?

The main village in the territory, Gurumsarai, was closed to the outside world. Strangers happening upon the village were immediately carted off to hard labor. Villagers were afraid to walk their own streets, fearful of suffering the same fate. Those caught trying to escape were tortured and, if not killed, were consigned to Adylov's slave labor crew.

Adylov milked the state budget he controlled. Tens of millions of rubles disappeared, while he and his multitudinous henchmen luxuriated in palaces eating caviar and the finest meats, consorted with concubines, and drove imported cars. He had 15 villas and 50 thoroughbred race horses. Adylov's crime network extended across Uzbekistan and into western Siberia, the Baltic region, and Moscow.[7]

People who resisted or tried to report on the situation to outside authorities were often at first wined and dined, but if they continued to speak out, thugs would step in to inflict broken bones, dismemberment, a slow death in a dank dungeon, or a quick blast from the barrel of a sawed-off shotgun.

Adylov is no isolated example of communism run amok. He is more the rule than the exception. The Soviet press describes deeply entrenched crime networks in Kazakhstan, Azerbaijan, Ukraine, and even Moscow itself. Operations of these networks dwarf those of the most sophisticated Western gangs. For Soviet robber barons, political power, violence, and booty are a way of life.[8]

A depraved breed of rulers thrives all over the country, enjoying unaccountable power rivaling that of the satraps of Persia or the khans of Asia. Lenin's dictum (that the party is unconstrained by law) originally set the stage for empowerment of the unscrupulous. Party members' activities became subject to scrutiny only from the top leaders, who judged members by no objective standard but

[7]Vladimir Sokolov, "Zone of Silence," *Literaturnaya Gazeta*, January 20, 1988, p. 13; article compiling readers' responses to Adylov case, and interview with B. Ye. Sviderskiy, "We Will Not Keep Quiet," *Literaturnaya Gazeta*, August 3, 1988, p. 13.

[8]Vladimir Sokolov, "Gang Rule," *Literaturnaya Gazeta*, August 17, 1988, p. 13.

91

according to whatever arbitrarily suited their purposes of the moment. As early as 1921, accounts denounced some party members' "extraordinary abuse of their privileged position for their own material advancement,"[9] and Stalin derisively referred to them as an "order of knights." Stalin himself placed legions of corrupt degenerates in responsible positions, while holding their lust for power in check by sheer force of terror. When the Stalinist terror ended, officials were able to turn unhindered to the quest for personal power. Over time, the "khanates" gained so much power that the Soviet Union is in danger of collapsing from within.

What the reform movement, in fact, boils down to is a civil war between those party members who want to resurrect the economy and save the system along with Soviet world power, and those robber barons who are battling to preserve their rule of territories and spheres of influence without interference from above.

Gorbachev and his followers see the institutionalized fiefdoms as a threat to the Soviet state. The Kremlin wants to prevent the country from degenerating into a patchwork of khanates. The main battle is political—how to wrest power away from the satraps and recentralize authority, while at the same time stimulating workers to produce.

To an astonished country, at the special Communist Party Conference in July 1988, Gorbachev outlined the transformation of the rubber-stamp Supreme Soviet into a two-chamber congress that would directly elect the nation's leader and promulgate legislation. Giving the soviets real power is a shrewd effort to build a base of support to counter the fiefdoms and to overhaul the economy.

By empowering the soviets, Gorbachev is creating an alternative governing mechanism to the Communist Party. The soviets have existed since Lenin's time. Local and regional soviets also exist, in addition to the Supreme Soviet. To give legislative independence to the Supreme Soviet, Gorbachev permitted contested elections of people's deputies, who in turn selected the members of the Supreme Soviet and the President. In 1990, contested elections have been extended to the regional and municipal soviets.

In successive elections, Gorbachev has achieved some success in ousting the robber barons. During the 1989 elections for seats in

[9]Aron Stolts in *Pravda*, November 12, 1921.

the new Congress of People's Deputies, some reformers were boosted at the expense of the *apparatchiks*. A total of 34 regional party secretaries were defeated, not a large measure of success considering that there are 1,500 electoral districts. In a highly publicized triumph for perestroika, however, maverick reformer Boris Yeltsin won a seat in Moscow with 89 percent of the vote. Timely leaks from the Central Committee denouncing him as an anticommunist and accusing him of departing from the party line greatly helped his campaign. He won on a platform railing against the corruption and special privileges of the party. In Estonia and Lithuania, nationalist reformers beat entrenched party bosses. In most regions, however, the same old party princes controlled the elections and got their men in office, countermanding orders from the top that new faces be introduced. Such an outcome demonstrated the weakness of central authority in the Soviet Union.

In 1990 elections further boosted the reformers. They captured the mayoralties of Moscow and Leningrad. Yeltsin won the presidency of the Russian Republic. In Lithuania the Sajudis Popular Front, which led the drive for independence, swept the elections. On February 25, 1990, from Siberia to the Georgian Republic, hundreds of thousands of people rallied for democracy and the ouster of Communist Party leaders. In Moscow alone, over 50,000 people marched, demanding participatory democracy. In July the Communist Party Congress indicated that communism is a spent political force.

At every opportunity, Gorbachev uses the turmoil resulting from the reforms to further his own aims. The massive strikes by miners during the summer of 1989, which he called a greater challenge to the leadership than even the Chernobyl disaster, provided the occasion for Gorbachev to call for early elections in the local soviets. In order to oust local party officials unresponsive to the people's demands, he said that the country's 15 republics were free to hold the elections as early as the fall of 1989.

Currently, Gorbachev stands at the top of both the old and the new political structures. As the General Secretary of the Communist Party, he has the strongest voice in the Politburo and the Central Committee, traditionally the governing and decisionmaking bodies. As President he heads the newly empowered electoral politics inaugurated with the election of the people's deputies.

The upheavals from liberalization could conceivably lead to Gorbachev's ouster from the leadership of the Communist Party, yet leave him as President of the country with his electoral base in the people's deputies, or vice versa. At that point the conflict inherent in the dual political structure would break out in the open with Gorbachev and a rival contending for supremacy. Indeed, a rumor that Gorbachev would resign as General Secretary and keep his position as President of the Supreme Soviet flew around in the world in January 1990, prompting Gorbachev to issue an official disclaimer.

Despite appearances and contrary to popular opinion in the West, Gorbachev's main goal is more complex than just to democratize Russia, though that may be a result of his efforts to create a more effective society. Gorbachev's career took off under Leonid Brezhnev, when he was promoted through the party ranks and nominated for nonvoting Politburo membership in 1979. Also a protégé of Yuri Andropov, he became a full-fledged Politburo member in 1980. Gorbachev is trying to save the Soviet state from centrifugal forces. His call for a rule of law is part of his effort to recentralize power. If activities of robber baron apparatchiks were subject to law, the top leadership would have more control over the country than it does at present. Of course, a rule of law can lead to a more democratic society.

Dispelling any lingering notions of decentralization at the top, Gorbachev has moved forcefully to consolidate power in his person. He has used his dual posts to oust his rivals at every opportunity, at the same time advancing his allies. A clear example of this trend is Gorbachev's April 1989 purge of 74 members of the Central Committee along with other top officials, whom he characterized as "dead souls."

The constitution produced by the regime in support of Gorbachev's effort to reassert political control has been criticized for centralizing too much power in the person of the General Secretary. The now-deceased Soviet physicist and dissident Andrei Sakharov warned of a return to Stalinism and declared, "A head of state with such powers in a country that does not have a multiparty system is just insanity." The government newspaper *Izvestiya*, however, said that "executive power is clearly weak now and not very active"

94

and argued that "the country needs a president with full rights."[10] In February 1990, Gorbachev lobbied for increased presidential powers and got them.

According to Gorbachev's advisers, he concluded that many Communist Party members are innovative, get-ahead types that the country needs in leadership roles, but that the party mechanism itself was corrupting—thus squandering the human capital. His policy of glasnost, translated as publicity or openness, was designed to liberate political leadership from a corrupt process. Glasnost has also served Gorbachev by exposing officials resisting change and by stimulating the population to think freely and to become more creative and productive in their jobs.

Gorbachev is the first leader of the Soviet Union with a university education. He stands out from his predecessors, most of whom were, in one top economist's opinion, "complete fools with a worm's view of the world and a poor understanding of their job."[11] Possessed of a keen analytical ability, Gorbachev has freed his mind from ossified ideology, and he has set about challenging the unsuccessful social and economic institutions that he has inherited. The many obvious failures of the Soviet system, together with the frustrations these failures have engendered, even among members of the Communist Party, have given Gorbachev reform opportunities that were unthinkable a decade ago.

Gorbachev's advisers report that he has become more radical during his tenure as he realizes the profound nature of the problems faced by the Soviet Union. They contend that after his first, limited attempts at reforming the system, Gorbachev has come to accept that the entire system will have to be dismantled if the Soviet Union is to survive as a world power. He is taking broad steps to revive the moral, political, and economic basis for society.

The Revival of Morality

Gorbachev believes that 70 years of unaccountable, arbitrary power has stripped Soviet citizens of moral and ethical codes by which to live. Moreover, communism has indoctrinated people

[10]"Does the Power Have Enough Power?" unattributed, *Izvestiya*, February 5, 1990, morning ed., p. 2.

[11]Abel Aganbegyan, *Inside Perestroika: The Future of the Soviet Economy*, translated by Helen Szamuely (New York: Harper & Row, 1989), p. 143.

against individual achievement and initiative and has bred passivity and mediocrity into the system. Gorbachev knows that these are not the characteristics of risk-takers and leaders, and he understands that envy blocks the progress of his economic reforms.

For instance, the key initiative to push private cooperatives to the forefront of the economy is meeting with resistance among the people. *Pravda* correspondents Y. Arakelyan and V. Somov found it necessary to devote an article of some length to explaining why citizens should not envy the owner of a successful dairy cooperative. They wrote:

> Evidently many people have not yet managed to overcome their prejudice against the "private businessman" as a money-grubber. Through this prejudice, as through a curtain of fog, they fail to see the most important thing—the enormous potential for using the help of cooperatives to fill the market with goods people need, including food products.[12]

Envious of their success and suspicious of entrepreneurship, citizens regard cooperative owners as less than respectable, with some people considering them fair game for attack.

Cases have been cited in the Soviet press of cooperative restaurants burned to the ground and livestock of cooperative farmers stolen as a result of envy of personal success. Even though consumers are accustomed to paying high black market prices, many are angered by the high legal prices charged by cooperatives. The Soviet consumer seems to think that cooperatives should supply black market quality goods at unrealistically low state prices.

Simultaneously, the crime empires prey on the newly formed cooperatives. The weekly *Moskovskiye Novosti* reported that mobsters demanded 50,000 rubles from the director of the Swallow Cooperative Bakery, threatening to kill members of his family if the money was not forthcoming. Thugs extort protection payments from taxi drivers at the Vnukovo Airport, south of Moscow, brandishing threats of harm to the drivers' families and destruction of their cars. In January 1989, the café manager and several patrons of the cooperative restaurant called "Come In and Try It" were stabbed by three unidentified assailants who firebombed the café.

---

[12]Yu. Arakelyan and V. Somov, "Farmers: Family Cooperatives Can Make a Noticeable Contribution to Food Resources," *Pravda*, January 14, 1988, p. 2.

The hapless co-op director would not name the perpetrators but said that, when he rebuilds the place, he should call the main dining room "Racketeers' Hall."[13]

Accustomed to stealing from state firms, Soviets think nothing of stealing from private ones. Co-op directors must pay bribes at every turn to receive supplies. One director attested that "if you are not into bribery, no one will talk to you." Exhausted by efforts to resist corruption, another concluded: "The dream of an honest private business has died."[14] The lack of a rule of law in the Soviet Union precludes the police from coming to the aid of private business people because Soviet law enforcement agencies themselves are riddled with corruption. This problem makes it difficult for Gorbachev to install market legality in the Soviet Union and to free vast slices of the economy from a grasping violence.

Still, some cooperative owners refuse to give up without a fight. Recently, 62 cooperative owners formed an association to try to protect themselves from hostility from the population and from marauding robber barons. Private taxi drivers are also taking matters into their own hands. One thousand drivers met recently in Vnukovo Airport to decide how to resist demands for protection money.

Gorbachev realizes that a rule of law and the revival of moral standards are critical to the success of the Soviet economy. At the plenary session of the Communist Party of the Soviet Union (CPSU) Central Committee on February 18, 1988, Gorbachev said: "Our economic reform, the development of the processes of democratization and openness, the renewal of the spiritual and moral sphere are links in a single chain." Four months later at the 19th CPSU Conference on June 29, 1988, Gorbachev spoke of the need to revive the "moral values, which have over the course of centuries been worked out by peoples and pooled and elaborated by the great minds of mankind." He has a ready answer to his critics: "Voices are heard talking about the collapse of spiritual and moral values. But it seems to me that what we are talking about is their revival."[15]

[13]David Remnick, "Violent Mobsters Strong-Arm New Soviet Cooperatives," *Washington Post*, February 12, 1989, p. A1.

[14]Ibid.

[15]"Increase the Intellectual Potential of Restructuring," speech by Mikhail Gorbachev before the CPSU Central Committee, *Pravda*, January 8, 1989, pp. 1–4, and *Izvestiya*, January 8, 1989, pp. 1–3.

These moral values include the revival of religion and independent standards of right and wrong. Bibles are now allowed in the country. According to Konstantin Kharchev, head of the government's Council on Religious Affairs, 1.2 million Bibles were imported in 1988. Couples are permitted to marry in religious ceremonies. The Soviet press even goes so far as to praise these ceremonies and to laud the existence of large numbers of communist believers. To emphasize the new religious tolerance, Gorbachev invited back to the Soviet Union a Christian sect that emigrated to Canada in the 19th century.

According to Valentin Falin, a foreign policy adviser to Gorbachev, about 50 to 60 million people in the Soviet Union profess allegiance to a church. Falin said that new churches and monasteries are being built and that religion does not belong to the past, but instead the hectic pace of modern life makes religion necessary. He said that the church "has played a positive role" in human history and added that believers do not work worse but "in many cases better than the atheists."[16]

Political Revival

To fight the inbred corruption, Gorbachev has opened to debate subjects that have been taboo for many years. Accounts of Stalin's atrocities are freely published, and the limits of glasnost are pushing ever outward. A Moscow magazine published a graphic conversation with Grigory Niazov, an ex-guard at a "special facility," a location where Stalin's victims were shot after they were summarily convicted:

> "We took them [the prisoners] about 12 kilometers, to a small hill. It was called Glukhaya [remote, secluded] Hill. There were hills all around, and we unloaded the prisoners right in the middle."
> "So you unloaded them and told them what their sentences were?"
> "Why tell them? We'd shout: 'Get out! Line up!' They'd climb out, and in front of them there was already a pit dug for them. They'd climb out, huddle together, and we'd immediately * * * "

[16]"Falin Speaks on 'Necessary' Role of Religion," *Die Welt*, Hamburg, Germany, November 14, 1988, p. 12.

"Were they silent?"

"Some were silent, some started to shout: 'But we're Communists, we're dying for no reason,' and other such things. But the women only cried and huddled closer together. So we immediately * * * "

"Was there a doctor with you?"

"Why would we need a doctor? We shot them, and if anyone was still moving, we would finish them off and get back in the trucks."[17]

Independent groups are springing up to set the record straight. One of these, called Memorial, has organized a successful nationwide campaign to honor Stalin's victims. Communist Party members who were arbitrarily stripped of their party membership and persecuted during Stalin's purges are being reinstated, often posthumously, as in the case of Nikolai Bukharin, the most famous victim of the 1938 show trial. He was rehabilitated in 1988. The Soviet government has even admitted the existence of the 1939 Hitler-Stalin pact, which handed over the Baltic republics to the Soviet Union, and Foreign Minister Eduard Shevardnadze declared the invasion of Afghanistan and the nine-year Soviet military role there illegal and immoral.

People are taking advantage of glasnost to oust corrupt party officials across the country. Recently, outraged residents of the city of Volgograd, who are forced to wait 10 years for desperately needed housing and to endure long lines daily for basic necessities, took to the streets and forced the ouster of the local Communist Party chief, who had obtained a desirable apartment for his daughter. The same story is being repeated across the country. In January 1990, the party chief of the Siberian city of Tyumen, described as a "feudal lord," was thrown out. Party leaders in the Soviet Far East and in Chernovtsy in the Ukraine were recently dumped for abusing their positions.[18]

The political debate has led directly to an open rejection of the Communist Party and a demand for participatory democracy. In

[17]Lev Razgon, "Carrying Out Orders," *Moskovskiye Novosti*, no. 48, November 27, 1988, p. 11.

[18]Esther Fein, "Angry Politics in the Soviet Heartland," *New York Times*, February 15, 1990, p. A18.

February 1990, the Communist Party took the previously unthinkable action of repudiating Article 6 of the Soviet Constitution, which had prohibited any political organizations other than the Communist Party. The regime itself has acknowledged that its tenure has been marked by lawlessness. As the ugly communist history has increasingly come to light, some party members have destroyed their membership cards in acts of revulsion.

Economic Revival

In early 1990, economic reforms were stalled because of their limited nature. Measures to provide incentives to cooperatives and long-term leasing of land to farmers, the most far-reaching reforms implemented to date, were confronting serious setbacks. However, there was cause for optimism. On February 7, 1990, the Communist Party included in its platform an endorsement of private property in the means of production.

To date, despite the calls from Gorbachev, his chief economic adviser Abel Aganbegyan, and deputy prime minister Leonid Abalkin for a broad overhaul of the economy, the majority of proposals that have actually been implemented amount to little more than cosmetic reforms.

A case in point is the program to decentralize decisionmaking in the economy by preventing officials from issuing instructions on day-to-day management of firms. Ministry planners are instructed to merely formulate broad directives for each enterprise, stipulating the proportions of financial accounts, wage accounts, investment, and final output, among other indicators. This instruction is an attempt to stop the deluge of contradictory orders from above and to give managers of enterprises the ability to relate their production to consumer demand. Managers are to use the plan instructions only as parameters.

This reform is aimed at gradually weeding out the gross output indicator as a measure of production. Two top economists, Aganbegyan and Abalkin, have expressed the opinion that firms should be able to ignore the directives from above in favor of orders from consumers.

The gross output indicator cannot be curtailed on a piecemeal basis. It has to be surgically removed. As long as a plan sets targets, Soviet managers will concentrate on fulfilling the indices that maximize their income while ignoring the others. Simply reducing the number of directives cannot improve an economic performance that is based on gross output. Despite the whirlwind of reform talk, the planning apparatus survives intact so far.

Pravda correspondent A. Cherepanov observed that firms that switch to self-financing and full economic accountability still cannot overcome "the inertia of the 'gross output' approach." Citing one case, he pointed out that the metalworkers of the Zlatoust firm wasted 25,000 metric tons of rolled metal to fulfill only 98.2 percent of their plan.[19] Similar stories abound in the Soviet press, demonstrating that the reforms have not led to increased efficiency and conservation of materials.

In 1989, Aganbegyan complained:

> For the moment the administrative system is still more powerful and still influences our enterprises and society at large. This influence is exerted not only through the old economic forms—the old price system, the centralized supply system, the various limits dictated from above, and so on—but also through some of the new forms. The administrative system has temporarily invaded the newly created economic system of management.[20]

Focusing on specifics, Aganbegyan reveals that reforms undertaken in the auto, toolmaking, and oil refining and processing industries had the result that "the norms simply expressed in a different form the old schedule of commands under the five-year plan." Not surprisingly, the enterprises performed no better than their counterparts in the same industries that had not been transferred to the reformed system of operation.[21]

Another expressed aim of the leadership is to release enterprises from centralized control in order to eventually make them self-financing. Since the Bolshevik Revolution, Soviet enterprises have been heavily subsidized by the state. To stem the drain on the national budget, Gorbachev has announced that all enterprises must become self-financing as soon as possible. In a departure from the past, he suggests that firms that fail to support themselves be

[19]A. Cherepanov, "They Looked at Themselves," *Pravda*, January 14, 1988, p. 1.

[20]Aganbegyan, *Inside Perestroika*, p. 164.

[21]Aganbegyan, *The Economic Challenge of Perestroika* (Bloomington and Indianapolis: Indiana University Press, 1988), p. 115.

allowed to go bankrupt. This move would force displaced laborers to seek jobs at more efficient firms.

So far this suggestion has been more intention than result. Officials proclaim that large numbers of enterprises have transferred to the self-financing system, when in fact most continue to receive subsidies as before.

A major goal of the reform program is to improve workers' living standards in order to motivate them to higher productivity. This goal requires upgrading the quality of manufactured consumer goods. In line with this new emphasis, the ministries' inspection staffs for quality control have been beefed up. However, since the gross output system remains in place, closer inspection has led to more rejections rather than to higher quality production. P. Shakh, chief engineer of a chemical machine manufacturing plant in Kiev, says that the result is to expand the unofficial economy:

> Every inspection, whether short or long, takes time away from the very specialists who ought to be working. Time is wasted on proving why the specifications say one thing rather than another, although those specifications were drawn up by an industry institute and reviewed by all the appropriate authorities. You have to explain why some piece of equipment isn't working, although everyone knows you'll reach retirement age before you're given any instruments for repair and maintenance needs. . . .
>
> Right now we have a paradox. An inspector sees and understands that an enterprise can't solve some problem, because it has neither the forces, nor the funds, nor the opportunity, but in his orders he writes the matter down and sets a harsh deadline. What can you do? You have to seek out "gray market" private contractors by hook or by crook and keep your own unofficial workers to get the job done.[22]

Another major stated goal of the reforms is to make production efficient. Soviet production wastes vast quantities of resources. Soviet firms use two and one-half to three times more resources than American firms to produce the same amount of output.[23] The scale of waste is truly astounding, and it frightens the leadership.

---

[22]P. Shakh, "Confessions of a Chief Engineer," *Pravda*, June 5, 1987, p. 3.

[23]Aganbegyan, *The Economic Challenge of Perestroika*, p. 39.

No longer can iron ore, oil, and coal be as cheaply extracted as in the past. Massive waste has led to exhaustion of easily accessible deposits, and the leaders are countenancing the thought that they may have to import oil and raw materials in the future. The present strategy is aimed at increasing efficiency within the existing system. Much of the effort to increase efficiency is focused on superficial measures, such as administrative ways that decrease the capital-output ratio and leasing systems that leave the planning apparatus intact. Indeed, volumes of ink are devoted to the concept of leasing, which in Aganbegyan's view is the "highest form of contract agreement . . . because only then do the means of production definitely pass over into the possession, use, and management of the workforce." The problem, he goes on to point out, is that the owners "will not be full owners, merely the managers, and will not be able to sell them and share the proceeds."[24] Moreover, Aganbegyan says,

> It is not in the manager's direct interest to move sections of his workforce over to a system of contract agreements. If the teams work well, the workers will receive more money. But the managers receive nothing extra, though the new system brings them more work.[25]

Price reform is another key element in the reform program. Prices have been fixed at the same level since 1967. It is true that Soviet firms often get around this and manage to increase prices by slightly altering a product and calling it new. Still, prices do not reflect market values. The true value of goods is evident in the speed with which goods disappear from store shelves and are snapped up by the black market or remain unsold. The leadership maintains that irrational prices are to blame for shortages in the economy. However, efforts to set new, better prices cannot meet the dynamic requirements of supply and demand. Prices cannot reflect the scarcity or utility of resources unless they are set by markets; until they are, production will remain disorganized.

The long-term goal is to free prices of most products to reach their market levels. In the meantime, the flourishing black market, where market prices already hold, has taken the initiative away

[24]Aganbegyan, *Inside Perestroika*, pp. 76–77.
[25]Ibid., p. 81.

from the Kremlin. However, black market prices are higher than under legally sanctioned markets, because of the inherent risks and difficulties of illegal operation.

Some reformers see price reform in terms of setting higher prices to absorb excess purchasing power and to allow producers of fuel and raw materials to become self-financing. Currently, these inputs are subsidized as a spur to final outputs, resulting in the squandering of resources. Aganbegyan says that price reform does not yet mean market pricing: "As we carry out the price reform in 1990, the majority of the prices will still be set centrally."[26] Those that are not set centrally are to be set by republican and local organizations. Floating and contractual prices are for the future—"if we master the economic methods of market regulation and the principles of socialist competition, and if we liquidate production and trade monopolies."[27] Even then the state will "regulate prices by establishing the working rules for free and contractual pricing. We shall want to avoid deliberate and unnecessary price rises leading to extortionate profits."[28] This statement suggests that reformers do not understand that price rises, leading to excess profits, are the signal to expand production.

Retail price reform is even less promising. Aganbegyan says that a kilo of meat priced at 1.8 rubles in the state shops carries a subsidy of 3.5 rubles. The nonsubsidized price would rise to 5.3 rubles—a tripling of prices, which, he says, cannot happen. Moreover,

> Many people have grown used to and accept the existing situation of shortages in the meat and dairy trade. They accept that the state shops offer an extremely small choice of goods. Many people have never known or even seen anything else.[29]

The leadership plans to reset official prices over a period of years, while permitting nonstrategic goods to seek market levels. But "strategic" can be defined broadly by those who resist reform.

This approach to price reform will not work. Firms cannot discover the right prices without input from consumers. This halfway

[26]Ibid., p. 29.
[27]Ibid., p. 29.
[28]Ibid., p. 48.
[29]Ibid., p. 27.

approach will serve only to further distort an already irrational pricing system and will lead to more confusion and shortages. For a profit system to work, prices must reflect true market values. This means prices must be free, and if prices are free, resources must be free to follow the movements of prices. Investments have to move in the direction of profits and away from losses. This change cannot happen unless property rights are assigned. Economists can speak abstractly about simulating profit models, but bureaucrats cannot perform the functions of owners.

Exaggerated claims have been made for the success of reforms. In his 1989 book, Aganbegyan contended that

> the new economic conditions introduced at the beginning of 1988 have speeded up the production of consumer goods, the dynamics of commodity circulation and of paid services by one and a half times compared with the same period in the previous year. . . . For the first time since 1978 we have managed to increase the GNP of the country by 5 percent and the use of consumer goods and services by 7.5 percent.[30]

This conclusion is wishful thinking, as all Soviet press reports stress the worsening shortages of consumer goods. Indeed, in September 1989, *Pravda* reported that out of 276 basic consumer goods, 243 cannot be found in shops, including soap, toothpaste, razor blades, notebooks, shoes, and clothing. In 1990 Moscow prohibited provincial residents from traveling to the capital to buy scarce goods. Leningrad authorities had already taken such action. Moreover, reports from the Soviet Union do not add up to an economy that is growing at a 5 percent clip. On the contrary, all signs point to a continuing slide.

In 1988, Aganbegyan redefined the "socialist principle of distribution" to include merit pay: "Now salary levels are more closely linked to the quality and quantity of work, following the basic socialist principle of distribution."[31] The sentiment is good. However, the continuing stream of articles in the Soviet press attests to

[30]Ibid., p. 9.

[31]Gorbachev turned the socialist motto on its head with his "From each according to his ability; to each according to his work." Since Marx, it had been "From each according to his ability; to each according to his needs." Aganbegyan, *The Economic Challenge of Perestroika*, p. 19.

the fact that salary levels do not correspond to contributions to the economy. In a recent issue of the Moscow magazine, *Sotsialisticheskaya Industriya*, economist Pavel Bunish, a supporter of perestroika, lamented: "Self-financing, self-government, and self-planning virtually do not exist."[32]

Before betting too heavily on the success of perestroika, the West should wait for two telltale signs: the Soviets must substitute profitability for gross output targets as the criterion for managerial success, and private property must become a reality. There is no prospect of reforming the Soviet economy as long as it is guided by the perverse incentives of the gross output indicator.

The other main source of distorted incentives stems from the absence of private property. The Soviet Union simply lacks the economic and social institutions that would allow it to use physical and human capital efficiently. Since, in effect, no one owns anything, capital and the means of production are not used in ways that produce maximum results. Peasants working on collective farms are not going to work as hard or as thoughtfully as a farmer on his private land. And bureaucrats in Moscow will not allocate capital as efficiently as the capitalist whose wealth depends upon his investment skills.

Gorbachev and his supporters have distanced themselves—in words—from the failed Soviet economy. As early as 1987, Gorbachev declared that "the essence of what we plan to do throughout the country is to replace predominantly administrative methods by predominantly economic methods."[33] Yet, the gross output system continues to prevail over economic methods.

Gorbachev can overcome the irrationality that plagues his economy only if he abolishes the gross output targets and makes profit the basis for rewarding managers. But even profits are not an incentive unless they can be invested with benefits accruing to those who earn them. Such investments require private property.

Hungarian economist Tibor Liska, aware of the need to replace socialist ideology with private property incentives, has suggested auctioning the use of state-owned property to the highest bidder,

---

[32]In Martin Sieff, "Gorbachev's Reforms Lose to Possibility of Power Struggle," *Washington Times*, March 13, 1989, p. A8.

[33]Mikhail Gorbachev, *Perestroika: New Thinking for Our Country and the World* (New York: Harper & Row, 1987), p. 74.

with the government collecting rents from leases held by private individuals.[34] However, this solution cannot work, because it does not solve the investment problem. Managers of leased factories or leased farms have no incentive to invest their profits in expansion of the factory or investment in the land because the property is not theirs but the state's. Without ownership rights, the allocation of investments toward profitable activities and away from losses cannot take place. Indeed, in a lease system managers can find that it is not in their interest for the state to invest in expanding production, because expansion could drive down their profit margin. As long as they do not have to worry about a rival organizing a new factory and bringing competition (that is, as long as there is no private property), they may find that they have the incentive of a monopolist to restrict output.

In the fall of 1989, economic reform took a step back. In November, Deputy Prime Minister Leonid Abalkin announced an ambitious reform program that was designed to gradually phase in a market economy. Proposals included selling off some state enterprises, establishing a financial market in the Soviet Union, freeing some prices to reach market levels, and developing a currency market that would lead to partial convertibility of the ruble. During that same month, however, Abalkin himself announced emergency measures that amounted to a continuation of planning, saying that "rigid state orders" will be reimposed on the production of some foodstuffs and basic household necessities that are in dangerously short supply.

Abalkin's reform program of November 1989, a compromise in itself, was not approved. The prevailing public mood of anger over higher prices and over worsening shortages of consumer goods led instead to the adoption, in December 1989, of the Ryzhkov Plan, a continuation of the system of administrative planning focused on increasing the production of consumer goods. This plan maintains controls over the economy until at least 1993, the midpoint of the five-year plan.

It is understandable that the Soviet leader would wish to proceed cautiously in overhauling the economy, but the experience of piecemeal reforms has not been encouraging. They seem to have made

[34] See "Into Entrepreneurial Socialism," The Economist, March 19, 1983, p. 23.

the economic crisis worse. Examples are numerous. For instance, the self-financing of enterprises, called for in the 1987 Law on Enterprises, sought to reduce the dependence of Soviet firms on subsidies. In practice the law has had the opposite effect. Factories have awarded workers pay raises prior to an increase in productivity. The result has been increased subsidies in many instances, with the money supply increasing while output lags. The government has responded by slapping new regulations on the enterprises, thereby increasing the confusion.

In another instance, restrictions on the size and number of cooperatives and private farms have held down competition, thus allowing a relatively small number of businesses to charge high prices without appreciably increasing the supply of goods. Consumer outrage at such high prices has, in turn, encouraged the government to tax and regulate the businesses, while banning some types altogether. Yaroslav Kuzminov, a senior scientific associate at the USSR Academy of Sciences Institute of Economics, complains that

> with one hand we are trying to bring into play the normal economic laws based on rational behavior, while with the other we wave angrily at people who have started to act within the framework of these new laws. But once the particular interests of the particular owner have been liberated, then we should not just wave our hands but create competition for him.[35]

The new Soviet government is stumbling toward private property in agriculture in unpromising ways. On February 28, 1990, the legislature passed a law that requires local governments and heads of collective farms to lease land to individuals for farming, home construction, country houses, day-care centers, sports centers, and small businesses. The law specifies that these leases can be hereditary within the family but cannot be sold or sublet—the land tenure conditions of feudalism.

It seems that the Soviet government intends to re-enact the historical transformation from feudalism to capitalism: first, private use-rights in the land, followed by the right to sublet, and finally the right to alienate or sell. Conceivably, the process could move rapidly if large numbers of people choose to exercise their new rights to

[35]Leontyeva, p. 2.

108

lease land. This move to property rights would compel local officials to let go of the best lands as well as the worst. However, a poll taken by the government newspaper *Izvestiya* indicated that only 12 percent of those surveyed intended to immediately take advantage of the new opportunity.

A go-slow attitude on the part of the peasants may doom the initiative. If only a few people apply, the worst land will be put in private farming. Moreover, the law allows the state to repossess the land if the lease-holder causes ecological damage or uses the land in a vaguely defined "unreasonable" way. Sociologist Tatyana Zaslavskaya, a member of the Congress of People's Deputies that passed the law, says,

> It's one thing to change laws and quite another to change the thinking and psychology of the people. No matter what Moscow says, local officials will do everything they can to save their own skins and their control over the land. The rural population is not educated or sophisticated and is frightened of the authorities that have always ruled over them.[36]

It is possible that within a year or less Gorbachev will argue that the leasing system has proved not to be sufficiently attractive to put land into private farming and that more radical steps must be taken. Already reform-minded newspapers, political groups, and economists are demanding more meaningful steps toward private property. In *Novy Mir*, economists Boris Pinsker and Larisa Piyesheva summed up the case:

> In competition over time, free farming and the enterprise economy have come out the winners, and many centuries of human experience show that freedom of the individual is not only the highest social value but also the most profitable way of organizing the life of society.[37]

In September 1989, Leonid Abalkin gave a severe assessment of perestroika's results:

---

[36]David Remnick,"Soviets Pass First Law Permitting Land Leasing," *Washington Post*, March 1, 1990, p. A1.

[37] Ibid.

The economic situation in the country has continued to deteriorate over the past 18–24 months. . . . So far we have not succeeded in halting the growth of negative processes. This applies particularly to the consumer market, the budget deficit, and monetary turnover. There is growing dissatisfaction with the progress of the reform and social tension is mounting.[38]

The worsening economic crisis increases the urgency for fundamental change. The chief danger of the half-hearted measures is that they use up Gorbachev's political capital for no practical purpose.

Faced with possible societal collapse, Soviet Premier Nikolai Ryzhkov told the Supreme Soviet in October 1989 that "the only way of creating an interest in highly productive and effective labor is through the interest arising from ownership." He went on to attribute "the imbalance of finances, the paucity of the consumer market, supermonopoly in the national economy, parasitism of plunderers and corrupting elements" to state ownership. Such admissions lead logically to privatizing the Soviet economy.

[38]Leonid Abalkin, interview in *Izvestiya*, September 23, 1989, p. 3.

6. Privatizing the Soviet Economy

The Soviet Union has proved that socialism does not work economically or socially. Today classical liberals (advocates of capitalism and personal freedom) find far more soulmates among Moscow's intelligentsia, to whom freedom is an exciting concept, than they can find on American university faculties or among the intellectuals ensconced in New York publishing houses, Hollywood, and U.S. television networks. In the West, intellectuals often dismiss economic freedom as "fascist." Others construe economic freedom as the right to entitlements that crowd out individual responsibility. In America today it is commonplace to see human rights arrayed in opposition to the right to be the majority shareholder in one's income.

In an editorial on New Year's Day 1989, the *New York Times* summed up the attitude toward Reagan's restoration of property rights and rescue of the U.S. economy from stagflation:

> Mr. Reagan asked the country to dream dreams, and it has. Yet as Hugh Heclo, a Harvard professor, noted in a recent essay, "these were necessarily dreams of private advantage, not public accomplishment." Just as he promised, Mr. Reagan's social gospel celebrated individualism. . . . It too easily tolerated money-grubbing. . . . There was virtually no talk about collective purpose, sacrifice, hard choices.

This negative attitude toward freedom is shared by the corporate bureaucracy that runs many Fortune 500 firms and megabuck foundations, and by economics professors who believe growth is impossible without a bureaucratic industrial policy. Like the Soviets, we, too, have a nomenklatura that uses government for its purposes. Organized special interests use the government to create economic rents (noncompetitive profits) for themselves. Acting through government officials and elected politicians, these interests maneuver to seize advantage from government programs, as the recent scandals at the Pentagon, the National Endowment for the

111

Arts, and the U.S. Department of Housing and Urban Development show. In the United States, use of the government's coercive power to solve every kind of societal problem—and in the process to curtail the liberties of the people—finds a ready constituency in the halls of Congress and in corporate board rooms.

The Western intellectual's hostility to economic freedom is a threat to Soviet economic liberalization. Soviet reformers complain that Western voices offset their own and confuse the Soviet government by insisting that planning is needed to make the market work and that property rights must be restricted in the interests of an equal distribution of income. The West, with its emphasis on social welfare and redistribution, discourages the Soviets from the incentives they so desperately need. Many Western economists, politicians, and business people believe the Soviet economy can be rescued with bank credits, technology, and the importation of turnkey factories. They do not believe that economic liberalism and the reform of social institutions are very important. To the contrary, many believe that planning and authoritarianism give the Soviet government the ability to make quick decisions and to override the various forms of opposition that sometimes delay new business ventures in the West.

With professors and influential business people clamoring for the United States to copy Japanese industrial policy, and with Congress's emphasis on distributional issues, the atmosphere is not conducive for the State Department or the administration to urge the efficacy of private property and market pricing on Soviet leaders. Moreover, the multilateral aid-giving institutions, which the United States organized and supports, have spent the post-war period touting planning and socialized investment as the cure for poverty and underdevelopment. The Third World debt crisis and falling living standards in less-developed countries have resulted from this mistaken approach.[1] Yet, we are now putting into place a development bank for Eastern Europe.

Unless there is a revolution in thinking in the West, these initiatives, like many in Africa and Latin America, are likely to produce lucrative fees and up-front profits for lenders, while deflecting the

[1]See Paul Craig Roberts, "Third World Debt: Legacy of Development Experts," *Cato Journal*, Vol. 7, no. 1, Spring/Summer 1987.

Soviets and Eastern Europeans from the true path of economic development. The availability of hard-currency financing will let politicians avoid difficult decisions and continue subsidies that misallocate scarce resources. Moreover, the external financing is likely to be distributed through political mechanisms, and the competition for these funds will be more remunerative than market activity. Real economic development will languish while rent-seeking activities flourish.

The admiration, still so prevalent in the West, for the interventionist state, will cause continuing hardships in the East. The Soviet economy is collapsing. Soviet economists say that if it is not radically reformed quickly, Soviet rulers will be faced with the inability of their society to feed the people.

To achieve an efficient economy, the Soviet Union must address the property problem. From the standpoint of the future, it makes little difference who the initial owners are. Historically in the West, the assignment of property rights took place in a long process over the course of centuries. The Soviets, however, do not have centuries. Throughout the Soviet Union, de facto property rights exist in the informal economy that everyone, including state firms, relies upon for provisions. These property rights could be recognized and given legal protection. Problems will no doubt arise where black market enterprises obtain their materials by theft from state supplies, but these past crimes will have to be forgiven while contractual relationships take the place of theft. Once property rights are assigned, the economy will become more efficient, and eventually the resources will find their way into the most efficient and productive hands.

It is a myth that capitalism perpetuates permanent income inequalities, making some families rich for all generations, while condemning those without property to perpetual squalor. In the United States it is easier to make money than to keep it. A vast number of firms make their living by trying to preserve and enlarge the capital of others, whether the fortunes of rich people or the pensions of factory workers or state employees. Even in the hands of professionals, the retention of wealth is a daunting task, because not even capitalists have rules that always ensure the correct allocation of capital. However, the capitalist rules do ensure that incorrect and wasteful misallocations cannot be permanently entrenched with subsidies until they bleed a nation dry.

113

The reason economic freedom works is that it does not tolerate and perpetuate mistakes. In the Soviet Union, mistakes have been made on a vast scale for three-quarters of a century. For the Soviet Union to extract itself from failed economic and social institutions is the great challenge of our time. After so many decades of mistakes, the Soviets have acquired a productive capacity that in many cases is not capable of producing an output with a value greater than the inputs. Therefore, there must be a tremendous write-down of the book values of capital assets in the Soviet Union. The only way an accurate calculation of asset values can take place is by privatizing the economy and permitting values to be established in the market.

The privatization of the Soviet economy is a challenging problem for which the world has no precedent. Countries such as Britain and Chile, which have privatized on a large scale, possessed state companies that, while inefficient and subsidized, operated under market pricing and produced marketable goods. Soviet firms lack these ties to market rationality. The irrational character of Soviet gross output deprives it of value on world markets. More fundamentally, Soviet firms lack efficient production functions and many firms are irrationally located, being far from their main sources of inputs. Some Soviet factories, if privatized, would have to be dismantled for their junk value.

To begin the process, the ownership of each factory could be distributed in shares to its workers and managers. The process will not permit an equal distribution across the Soviet Union, because values cannot be known until property rights are assigned and a capital market forms. In many cases people will have an intuitive sense of relative values, guided by the black market and the existing trade in stolen state goods. Obviously, some workers and managers are going to benefit from receiving more valuable shares than others. However, fairness cannot be made the criterion because that would require continuing redistributions that would disrupt the assignment of rights and violate the legal protection of property. It would not be an auspicious beginning if new property owners are stripped of part of their new holdings because the market establishes high values on their shares. If newly assigned rights are overturned in the interest of fairness, private property will be off to a shaky start.

The reform of the Soviet economy could founder on envy, the great enemy of the market. There will always be times when fortuitous events benefit some property owners to the disadvantage of others. However, it is not possible to overturn or to redress every distribution of the market without killing the market and the incentives of private property. Human beings are inventive and resourceful when they are placed in a climate that allows them to be. We see that easily in the United States where every year we benefit from a million or more new immigrants, most of whom are illegal. These masses of people from Third World countries do not build a reserve army of unemployed; they build productive and prosperous lives, because our social and economic institutions permit it. The value of these institutions, organized on the basis of private property, and their contribution to our society far outweigh distributional inequalities.

The property problem in the Soviet Union could be solved by a national lottery. However, a lottery would result in Soviet citizens owning shares in firms far distant from their homes. For a capitalist nation such as our own, the stock market keeps owners in touch with distant property, but in a country with no experience with private property, a stock market could be too abstract a basis upon which to resurrect private property. Moreover, since in most cases values would not be known at the time of the distribution, distant owners' suspicions would be inflamed in those cases where market valuations proved to be low. On the basis of their experience with Soviet life, the new owners would quite naturally suspect that their distant property was being stripped by those on the scene, leaving an empty, valueless shell.

For this reason alone, it would be better to privatize by making the workers and managers of each factory its owners. In this way, the new owners are on the scene to watch over their individual interests. Moreover, in those cases in which the enterprises are economically viable, the incentive of ownership will improve the operation of the factory.

The collective and state farms could also be divided among those people currently on the land. Many problems would no doubt arise in the distribution of buildings and equipment, but those problems would be minor compared to the collapse of the Soviet economy. The peasants and agricultural workers could elect someone in each locality to be in charge of privatization, with the runner-up responsible for reviewing the distribution of shares. Obviously, jealousies and disagreements could not be solved by distant decisionmakers.

Once property is distributed, prices must be freed all at once. A market economy cannot be established piecemeal, because values cannot be established unless all prices are free to adjust. The transformation will be unpleasant, but in an economy facing collapse, turmoil leading to improvement is preferable. Moreover, everyone will be kept jumping to adjust to the new system and to take advantage of its opportunities, leaving little time for opposition. To aid the process, the government would have to provide during the transition period some form of guaranteed income, unemployment insurance, or food stamps. Today in the Soviet Union, millions of people receive a low wage for which they have to do very little work, and there will naturally be resistance to being thrown upon one's own resources—especially before their values are clear. Workers in badly sited or equipped factories may find their labor unsalable in their present locations. Shares that they receive in local housing and in their factories or work places would have correspondingly low values. Therefore, the Soviet Union can privatize only with the aid of a social safety net. It goes without saying that this temporary safety net can provide scarcely more than subsistence.

For labor markets to adjust, all restraints on internal travel and choice of residence have to be removed.

The turmoil generated from the transformation of the Soviet economy could best be handled by permitting more political competition. In February 1990 the Communist Party leadership repudiated Article 6 of the Soviet Constitution, which guaranteed the leading role of the Communist Party. This fundamental change permits the rise of a multiparty system. Gorbachev realizes that it is difficult for a government to govern without free elections that provide feedback as to the success of its policies. Governing is not just the exercise of power, as Lenin thought. A one-party system deprives the government of information flows that are essential to efficient governance. More democracy will enable the government to better manage the privatization of the economy and the creation of free social and economic institutions.

The Soviet Union has proved conclusively that socialism does not work and that planning cannot supplant the market. No one can accuse the Soviet government of half-hearted efforts. No one can say that it did not have enough power, or enough bureaucracy, or enough planners, or that it failed to persevere or go far enough. The Leninist state went as far as it is possible to go. There were no private property rights, and there was no freedom.

Looking at the problems confronting the Soviet Union, we must marvel at the courage of Gorbachev and his supporters—though it is a courage partly born of necessity, even desperation, because the Soviet economy simply does not work. The failure of Soviet socialism was hidden for decades by the availability of vast quantities of easily accessible resources, and by a vast landscape, large seas, lakes, and fabled rivers to serve as reservoirs for industrial pollution. Now it is common to see estimates that the Soviet economy requires two and one-half times as many inputs per unit of output as the U.S. economy. Easily accessible resources are used up, making the inefficient production functions unworkable and unlivable. Moreover, destruction of the environment has led to rising mortality rates among all sectors of the population. According to Soviet economist Vladimir Tikhonov, only radical economic changes can prevent "famine in the very near future." Boris Yeltsin, the top vote-getter in the 1989 Soviet elections, predicted a "grassroots, spontaneous revolution" if the consumer's plight does not improve.

Despite the precarious position of the Soviet economy, privatization is an uncertain prospect. Gorbachev and his reform-minded supporters have recognized the material self-interest of the Communist Party as an impediment to necessary reforms. His decision to create new political structures in order to destroy the power of the party reflects the belief that the Communist Party cannot be won over to reform, but the Soviet people can.

This approach may be overly optimistic if a majority, or even a large minority, of the Soviet people do not favor private property and a market economy. Indeed, the fear and envy of the people have blocked Gorbachev's reforms as effectively as the refusal of communist apparatchiks to implement them. Soviet citizens have never had the primary responsibility for meeting their own economic needs. For a population not brought up to see life as the pursuit of opportunity, the fear of market uncertainty can be overwhelming. Moreover, from grade school forward, the people have heard the maxim, "from each according to his abilities, to each according to his needs." Their envious response to reforms permitting cooperatives and private farming forced Gorbachev to curtail many new incentives.

Gorbachev's problem is illustrated both by his low standing in Soviet polls and by a Soviet joke: "A genie appears to a downtrodden peasant and offers to grant his deepest wish. Without a pause, the peasant asks for the death of his neighbor's cow." We should learn something when Soviet Deputy Prime Minister Leonid Abalkin says that the new law permitting private property omits the actual words themselves because of the negative attitude of the Soviet people toward that concept.

Gorbachev could succeed in enhancing his power while stripping the party of its own, but it is unclear how effectively he can rule through the new political structure or convince elected bodies to take the country in directions it does not want to go. Although the Communist Party long ago ceased to be an ideological force, it remained a powerful vested interest. By stripping the party of its authority, Gorbachev may create a vacuum. One plausible outcome is chaos and the rise of a new ideological force.

Great Russian chauvinism might move to the fore. On ice for 70 years, today this native ideology resists Gorbachev's policies. The chauvinists have their own journals and, although not communists, they are angry with Gorbachev and reformers for trying to import a "decadent" foreign economic system into Mother Russia. They are also angered by rebellion in the republics and the loss of Eastern Europe. Large numbers of Russians are now returning to the motherland from the outlying republics that they were sent to colonize, and, like the French returning from Algeria, they are embittered. The loss of Russian prestige will feed the nationalism of the chauvinists.

Any worsening of the plight of the Soviet consumer will also work to the chauvinists' political advantage, and piecemeal reforms are almost certain to accentuate problems rather than solve them. Vasily Selyunin has compared Gorbachev's economic reforms to an effort to cross an abyss with two leaps.[2] This implies Gorbachev's

---

[2]Vasily Selyunin, "Sources," *Novy Mir*, May 1988.

failure, but because the chauvinists have no feasible economic policy of their own, their rise to power would not contribute to a solution of the Soviet Union's problems. However, it could confront the world with a dangerous and desperate Russian nationalism.

It would be premature in 1990 to write off democratic forces and the imperatives of economic rationality. Gorbachev or a successor may succeed in forming a more radical government that can infuse rational incentives into the Soviet economy. If not, the Soviet Union—and perhaps the world—can expect turmoil.

In April 1990 Soviet Foreign Minister Eduard Shevardnadze warned of "a social explosion capable of igniting not only the befogged minds but also the giant stockpiles of nuclear and chemical weapons and nuclear power stations and the zones already weakened by environmental and natural disasters and regions shaken by inter-ethnic strife."[3]

[3]Walter Friedenberg, "Shevardnadze Warns of 'Explosion,'" *Washington Times*, May 7, 1990, p. A1.

7. Beyond Marxism

The Communist Party has purged itself from power, and Gorbachev seems determined to purge socialism from the Soviet economy. With the party acknowledging the crimes and failures of its rule, perhaps we in the West can also move beyond Marxism and escape from our adversarial relationship with our own society, a relationship that has led many Westerners into shameful apologetics for Soviet communism.

The aspirations embodied in central planning convinced many people that the ends justified the means. Everything was permissible to advance the cause. Hesitancy to lie or to destroy those who stood in the way was intellectual squeamishness. The faint-hearted were reminded that "you can't make an omelet without breaking eggs," and the crimes of the day were dismissed as the necessary means to tomorrow's utopia. In his memoir, *The Education of a True Believer*, Lev Kopelev described how he participated in mercilessly stripping the peasants of food during the winter of 1932–33,

> scouring the countryside, searching for hidden grain, testing the earth with an iron rod for loose spots that might lead to buried grain. With the others, I emptied out the old folks' storage chests, stopping my ears to the children's crying and the women's wails. For I was convinced that I was accomplishing the great and necessary transformation of the countryside.[1]

Even after he witnessed the massive starvation during the terrible spring of 1933 and saw the earth littered with corpses, Kopelev did not lose faith. Neither did sympathetic Western intellectuals who supported Soviet communism with a half century of apologies and prevarications.

How did such an appalling betrayal of the truth and lack of realism take hold of professors from our finest universities, religious

[1]Lev Kopelev, *The Education of a True Believer* (New York: Harper & Row, 1977), pp. 11–12.

leaders, scientists, journalists, businessmen, and public officials? Part of the answer is that the judgment of experts and witnesses was distorted by a prevailing intellectual climate that cast suspicion on Western economic and social institutions and that placed inordinate hopes for humanity on coercive economic and social engineering in the Soviet Union.

The denigration of Western economic achievements has been an established trend since the time of the Industrial Revolution. T. S. Ashton of the University of London examined historians' treatment of capitalism and the Industrial Revolution.[2] He found that historians neglected general economic improvements and stressed specific horror stories. The life of the rural peasant was idealized; the living standards of the factory worker, deplored. The fact that factory workers did not return to the land despite the pessimism of historians did not convince observers that workers thought themselves better off.

The period of the Industrial Revolution saw a dramatic increase in longevity coupled with a sharp drop in infant mortality. Population growth soared. From 1750 to 1850, Britain's population tripled, from about 10 million in 1750 to approximately 30 million in 1850.[3] A burgeoning middle class arose, whose ranks were filled with prospering wage earners and capital-owning businessmen.

Unfortunate developments stemming from the inability of local governments to deal with the rapid growth—crowded tenements, unsanitary conditions, and prevalence of disease—were all erroneously blamed on the emergence of the machine and the rise in labor productivity it engendered. The true culprits were in large part government fiscal and monetary policies. Ashton explains:

> If the towns were ridden with disease, some at least of the responsibility lay with legislators who, by taxing windows, put a price on light and air and, by taxing bricks and tiles, discouraged the construction of drains and sewers.[4]

---

[2]T. S. Ashton, "The Treatment of Capitalism by Historians," in *Capitalism and the Historians* (Chicago: University of Chicago Press, 1954).

[3]R. R. Palmer and Joel Colton, *A History of the Modern World*, 5th ed. (New York: Alfred A. Knopf, 1978), p. 423.

[4]Ashton, p. 52.

In addition, heavy levies on building materials and the scarcity of credit often resulted in the choice of slipshod housing or no housing at all for the poor.

Moreover, reports of the time were often written by members of the upper classes who abhorred the influx of the common people into the cities, which in pre-industrial days had provided uncrowded, pleasant residence. Offended by the presence of coarse peasants and the degeneration of streets into filthy, trash-strewn causeways, the 19th-century literati put the worst possible face on the changes. Although it is true that laborers' work and living conditions were bad by the standards of the wealthy, they were an improvement over their former conditions in rural areas.

Similarly, the Great Depression of the 1930s was attributed to the failure of capitalism rather than to the failure of government economic policy.

Faulty perceptions of Western economic history helped to set the stage for the intellectual mindset that romanticized Marx and the Bolshevik Revolution. Western intellectuals, disillusioned with their own countries, dropped standards of professional objectivity in their portrayal of the Soviet regime. They failed to inform the public of its true nature. If our doctors and engineers were to fail on such a scale, malpractice suits would proliferate wildly. Yet alleged experts, who enjoyed the public's trust, could not even report accurately on the broad outlines of the communist political and social system, much less on details of the economy.

Sociologist Paul Hollander has compiled an extensive record of people from all walks of life—clergy, scholars, government officials—who hailed the Soviet Union as the new hope for mankind and as the creator of the first moral social system.[5] In analyzing what caused this phenomenon, Hollander found that alienation from their own societies predisposed intellectuals to look favorably on societies that seemed to be the antithesis of their own. Many years of analyzing and deploring their own society's flaws left intellectuals with a bitter taste for capitalism. As members of an open society, they protested in graphic detail the seamy side of life in their own countries, while averting their gaze from the horrors of the Soviet Union. American intellectuals especially expressed

[5]Paul Hollander, *Political Pilgrims* (New York: Harper & Row, 1981).

pained surprise at the gap between their social ideals and practices in their own country.

Hollander explains that for the intellectual the identity of the perpetrators of an atrocity, along with the identity of the victims, is most important. Of less concern is the nature of the act itself. Depending on whether they view the actors with sympathy or hatred, they will judge the act as good or evil.[6] Intellectuals express moral outrage at misdeeds committed by right-wing governments, but downplay, ignore, and "place into context" the wholesale slaughter of innocent people by left-wing dictators. Something is seriously amiss when Western intellectuals unleash intense moral outrage over six priests murdered in El Salvador, yet express few words of reproach about the slaughter of millions in the Soviet Union.

Michael Polanyi has argued that the root of this double standard lies in an inconsistency at the foundation of the Western intellectual frame of mind.[7] The 18th-century Enlightenment had two results that combined to produce a destructive formula. On the one hand, Christian moral fervor was secularized, which produced demands for the moral perfection of society. On the other hand, modern science called into question the reality of moral motives. From the one we get moral indignation, and from the other, moral skepticism. These two disparate tendencies can be reconciled only by a joint attack on existing society. One pre-empts existing society's defense, while the other focuses moral indignation against it.

Scientific skepticism did not kill off moral motives. Rather, it drove them into an inverted form. To defend our history and purposes in terms of moral achievement brings smiles of derision from modern sophisticates. They will object that a veil is being used to hide the real motives (such as power) and the real machinations of vested interests. People who are motivated by moral purposes find that moral expression is spared the suspicion of dishonesty only when it takes the form of accusations of immorality against existing society.

Polanyi believed that the tension between moral demands and moral skepticism was initially very beneficial. It produced many

[6] Hollander, p. 427.

[7] Michael Polanyi, "Beyond Nihilism," in *Knowing and Being*, edited by Marjorie Green (Chicago: University of Chicago Press, 1969), pp. 3–23.

social reforms and inspired art and literature. But the tension was unstable, and a reformist force became a denunciatory ethic that is destructive. And now, as Allan Bloom has shown, it has turned on its own mother—the Enlightenment itself.[8]

It is hard to be an intellectual and escape this frame of mind. It has a power and a logic of its own. Even in its mildest form, it requires one to be a constant critic of society, with the stress on correcting past failures and righting past wrongs. A country that relies on a self-critical posture as its means of achieving progress is forced to underplay its achievements. Inevitably, it is at war with itself. When the indictments of economists, political scientists, sociologists, historians, theologians, ecologists, and arms controllers are added together, the result is a total indictment of America. One of the most successful nations in history, the United States projects abroad the image of a country totally dissatisfied with itself.

Consider a typical member of the intellectual elite. His commitment to society is conditional upon changes in institutions and policies that he thinks are necessary to bring about the desired improvements. Therefore, his allegiance at any point in time is weak; to satisfy his desire for progress, he feels he must remain an opponent of existing society. He does not see his country's gifts of foreign aid as attesting to its moral sense; rather, the insufficient amount is evidence to him of greed and selfishness. He justifies foreign nationalization of his fellow citizens' property as a necessary remedy for neocolonial exploitation. A strong defense posture is not a justifiable response to an external threat, but is provocative and the cause of an arms race. He reminds the alarmist of America's own sins and chides him for indifference. On the domestic scene he champions the failures as victims of society, and he explains the successful in terms of ill-gotten gains.

Anyone who tries to focus on American achievements and successes runs afoul of the denunciatory ethic, which demands ever more corrections of wrongs. Adversaries, however, are spared the searing criticism, because to denounce opponents implies affirmation of one's own society—and that subjects one to the suspicion

[8]Allan Bloom, *The Closing of the American Mind* (New York: Simon and Schuster, 1987), pp. 25–43.

of dishonesty and to the status of an unsophisticate. An academic or media career cannot survive such suspicion and status.

In academic life today, any work that affirms our society smells of patriotism and implies a lack of objectivity, whereas anti-Americanism has positive connotations. Anti-Americanism implies broadmindedness, a person who can transcend the anachronism of narrow national interest to represent the world, humanity, and history's best impulses. Unlike patriots, anti-Americans claim the quality of objectivity because they can apply skepticism to their own country, without restraints, without holding something back for the good of their country.

The extreme alienation of modern intellectuals removes them from contact with practical realities and leaves them susceptible to ideas that undermine their own society. A penchant for reducing complex human experience and realities into simplified theories emerges—hence the attraction of Marxism. They criticize their society by finding perfection in its antithesis.

Hollander reports that many intellectuals heard kindred voices in Marxian denunciations of

> capitalistic greed and wastefulness, excessive military expenditures, racism, poverty, unemployment, the impoverishment of human relationships, the lack of community, the vulgar noises of advertising, the crudeness of commercial transactions—practically everything that is intensely disliked by the Western intellectual. How could he fail to find some sense of affinity with those who seemingly share his values, his likes and dislikes?[9]

The psychology of alienation and the denunciatory ethic prevailing in Western intellectual circles were not the only impediments, however, to a realistic assessment of the Soviet Union. Another reason that the world was not informed of the true nature of Marxism-Leninism-Stalinism was that many disinterested, objective scholars of the Soviet system failed to comprehend that the Leninist state was based on violence alone. In the West, Marx was perceived by many as a humanist and Marxism-Leninism was viewed as the use of the state to do good works.

[9]Hollander, p. 8.

It was a fundamental error to assume that, because Marx's work contains a concept of alienation, he was a humanist.[10] "Communists preach no morality at all," Marx declared characteristically in the *German Ideology*. As the Marxist philosopher Eugene Kamenka has noted,

> The rejection of any appeal to "abstract" moral principles was for many decades one of the best-known features of the work of Marx and Engels. Marxism was distinguished from utopian socialism precisely by reference to its *scientific* character, to its refusal to confront society with moral principles and moral appeals. . . . Throughout the remainder of his life Marx would object bitterly to any attempt to base a socialist program on "abstract" moral demands embodied in such terms as "justice," "equality," etc.[11]

By ruling out a humanist reliance on good will among men as a vehicle for social change, Marx left only violence as the mediator between class interests and as the force of history. The leading role given to violence leads logically to Leninism and Stalinism. Lenin found in Marx's denial of moral motives the justification for violence as the mediator between the government and the people. Possessing a keen understanding of the Leninist state, Stalin took the use of violence still further. He made it into the mediator between the party and its members.

Lenin announced that the new Soviet society would be built on the basis of the dictatorship of the Communist Party in all areas of life: "The scientific concept of dictatorship means neither more nor less than unlimited power, resting directly on force, not limited by any laws, nor any absolute rules. Nothing else but that."[12] This was a fantastic claim, elevating Soviet power beyond any constraint. Not even kings ruling by divine right had made such total claims.

---

[10]See Paul Craig Roberts and Matthew A. Stephenson, *Marx's Theory of Exchange, Alienation, and Crisis* (Stanford, Calif.: Hoover Institution Press, 1973), especially pp. 84–89.

[11]Eugene Kamenka, *Marxism and Ethics* (London: Macmillan, 1969), pp. 4–5.

[12]V. I. Lenin, "A Contribution to the History of the Question of the Dictatorship," October 20, 1920, *Collected Works*, 4th Russian ed. (London: Lawrence & Wishart, 1960–68), p. 326.

Lenin went far beyond the establishment of an authoritarian dictatorship, of which the world has seen many, by denying the independent existence of law, morality, science, literature, art, and the individual himself. Such a total claim was unintelligible to most Western observers.

The Leninist state destroyed the basis for independent thought. The will of the Communist Party reigned supreme and permitted no voluntary organizations or even independent family life. Truth, justice, law, and morality were whatever served the interests of the party. The Leninist state is totalitarian because there is no area it cannot reach and no independent standards in which a person can take refuge from the claims of the state.

Lenin's doctrine of violence was widely acknowledged by the Communist Party. For example, in 1928 Grigori Pyatakov, later a victim of the doctrine, recognized and approved it:

> According to Lenin the Communist Party is based on the principle of coercion which doesn't recognize any limitations or inhibitions. And the central idea of this principle of boundless coercion is not coercion by itself but the absence of any limitation whatsoever—moral, political, and even physical.[13]

By the time of Lenin's death, the major features of the Soviet system were in place: a totalitarian state enforced by the secret police, and based on the administrative planning apparatus and forced labor camps.

The Soviet Constitution of 1936 promised freedoms as extensive as those of Western democracies, but only "in accordance with the interests of the workers and for the purpose of strengthening the socialist system." The essence of the Soviet system was expounded in Article 6, which stated that the Communist Party is the "leading and guiding force of Soviet society." Article 6 did not give the Communist Party a mere political monopoly, nor did it merely place the party as supreme to other parties. It made the party supreme to law, to morality, to all forms of association, even to independence of thought. Broad-ranging powers of punishment were explicit in the Constitution: "Whoever seeks to weaken the socialist system is an enemy of the people."

[13]In Robert Conquest, *The Great Terror* (London: Macmillan, 1968), p. 128.

People who could not discern the fundamental nature of the Soviet system were able to convince themselves that the Soviet Union was a new civilization, replete with a model constitution, a model penal system, and a rule of law. They failed to grasp that the definition of communist morality was what served the party. Alienated from their own societies and seduced by the Communists' concept of utopia, many Western intellectuals either failed to perceive or covered up the extraordinary excesses and failures of the Soviet regime.

By the mid-1930s the progressive intelligentsia saw in Soviet communism a new civilization. American churchman Sherwood Eddy wrote in 1934:

> Russia has achieved what has hitherto been known only at rare periods of history, the experience of almost a whole people living under a unified philosophy of life. All life is focused in a central purpose. It is directed to a single high end and energized by such powerful and glowing motivation that life seems to have supreme significance. It releases a flood of joyous and strenuous activity.[14]

Preeminent educator John Dewey was moved to note that instead of a purely economic scheme, socialistic communism in Russia was an "intrinsically religious" movement. He grotesquely equated communism with Christianity: "I feel as if for the first time I might have some inkling of what may have been the moving spirit and force of primitive Christianity."[15] Hollander reports that utopia-seeking travelers carried with them the intense expectation and even certitude that they would find a far superior social system. Forsaking objective analysis, writers mistook their own deepest inner longings for Soviet reality.

Far from realizing the implications, educated people in the West enthusiastically embraced the Bolsheviks' plans and formed movements to emulate them. The movement to plan science in the United Kingdom had such popular appeal that distinguished scientists

---

[14]Sherwood Eddy, *Russia Today—What Can We Learn from It* (New York: Farrah & Rinehart, 1934), p. 177.

[15]John Dewey, *Impressions of Soviet Russia and the Revolutionary World, Mexico, China, Turkey* (New York: Bureau of Publications, Teachers College, Columbia University, 1964), pp. 100, 104, 105. First published in 1929.

such as Michael Polanyi found it necessary to spend years of their lives opposing a well-meaning effort to plan science for the betterment of society. Many scientists were so enamored of Soviet policies that Polanyi's question "How do you plan a creative discovery?" made no sense to them, and they were prepared to give up their scientific independence in the name of social betterment.

Such an atmosphere of fantasy prevailed that even the most dramatic events in Soviet history were denied and swept aside if they did not jibe with the observer's mental picture of the Soviet regime. The most atrocious acts of history largely escaped critical comment: millions of people murdered by genocidal famines, purges that wiped out the military and political leadership, show-trials of the heroes of the Bolshevik Revolution, and forced labor camps that devoured millions yearly.[16] News of these events was suppressed until the last possible moment. For years, progressive intellectuals in the West swallowed the Soviet propaganda line and repeated it to the public.

Sidney and Beatrice Webb, founders of the London School of Economics and Political Science, wrote a glowing assessment of the Soviet system in their 1,000-page book *Soviet Communism: A New Civilisation*. According to the Webbs, the Soviet Union was governed by an admirable constitution and legal system, respect for which led the Webbs to attack the "anti-communist rumor" that Stalin was a dictator:

> If we are invited to believe that Stalin is, in effect, a dictator, we may enquire whether he does, in fact, act in the way that dictators have usually acted?
> We have given particular attention to this point, collecting all the available evidence, and noting carefully the inferences to be drawn from the experience of the past eight years (1926–34). We do not think that the Party is governed by the will of a single person; or that Stalin is the sort of person to claim or desire such a position. He has himself very explicitly denied any such personal dictatorship in terms which, whether or not he is credited with sincerity, certainly accord with our own impression of the facts.[17]

[16]Conquest, *The Great Terror*.

[17]Sidney Webb and Beatrice Webb, *Soviet Communism: A New Civilisation*, 3rd edition in one vol. (New York: Longmans, Green, 1944), p. 334.

The Webbs, along with many others, ignored the implications of Leninism, which by its very nature required a dictator. By the 1940s there was no excuse for such ignorance. It was clear that Stalin had consolidated power into his own hands by eliminating all potential rivals. In 1938 he had had Bukharin shot. And over the years, membership in the Politburo had proved singularly dangerous: 16 out of 33 members had been officially murdered by 1941.[18] Even the wife of the Presidium's president had been arrested and sent to the Gulag. Military commanders were exterminated on a large scale, leaving a weak and disorganized Russian army that almost succumbed to German forces at the beginning of World War II. But all the Webbs could see was Stalin's selfless devotion to the Soviet regime.

The Webbs were not alone in their admiration of Stalin. After a meeting with the dictator, the Reverend Hewlett Johnson, Dean of Canterbury, wrote:

> When these fateful and restless years are past, and when historians have settled down quietly to weigh the facts, there is small doubt that Stalin will stand out as a giant among pigmies, the man who, unlike those smaller men who clutch at power for themselves, trained and guided that great family of peoples that we call the Soviet Union towards the right exercise of power, gladly surrendering to them a power which is really their own as their understanding and ability to use it increases.[19]

"Nothing," wrote Johnson, "strikes the visitor to the Soviet Union more forcibly than the absence of fear."[20]

Walter Duranty, Pulitzer Prize–winning reporter for the *New York Times*, supported the view that Stalin's Politburo formulated policy by consensus:

> To make a familiar comparison, the Politburo is like a first-class football team, say Notre Dame in the days of the Four Horsemen, and Stalin is their coach, Knute Rockne. Each member of the team has his specific position, and knows

[18]Conquest, *The Great Terror*, pp. 538–39.

[19]Hewlett Johnson, *The Soviet Power* (New York: Modern Age Books, 1940), pp. 309–10.

[20]Johnson, p. 187.

what to do in any team play. Dozens or scores of plays have been worked out beforehand for any possible contingency, but the team as a whole depends on the coach, relies upon him, and looks to him for their leadership and inspiration. With the significant difference that Rockne sat on the sidelines, whereas Stalin carries the ball.[21]

In 1986 Mikhail Heller and Aleksandr Nekrich, examining Stalin in the context of Leninism, gave a different portrayal of the dictator in their history of the Soviet Union. They observe that "Stalin began consolidating his power at once," making use of "every means to consolidate his power, including the art of medicine." They describe the fate of one hapless official, Commissar of War M. V. Frunze, who in October 1925 was ordered by the Politburo to undergo an operation. He never rose from the operating table and was replaced by Stalin's crony Voroshilov.[22]

Small wonder that observers who could not see the outlines of the totalitarian regime in Lenin also could not see a dictator in Stalin. Since the nature of the Leninist state eluded observers, so did its results. For example, the Webbs reported the government-directed efforts to crush the peasantry, culminating in the famine of 1932–33 and 7 million deaths, as follows:

> There seems to be no doubt that, in spite of a local rise in mortality in a few areas during certain months of 1931–32, amounting to a tiny percentage of the whole (as the result, as we have explained in our section on the Collective Farm, less of any failure of crops than of the refusal of peasants to sow or to reap), the general death-rate and the infantile mortality rate for the USSR as a whole have continued to decline, year by year, *at the rate actually greater than in most other countries in the world*.[23]

This was written at a time when, according to Boris Pasternak, "there was such inhuman, unimaginable misery, such a terrible disaster."[24]

[21]Walter Duranty, *Stalin and Co.: The Politburo—The Men Who Run Russia* (New York: William Sloane Associates, 1949), p. 91.

[22]Mikhail Heller and Aleksandr Nekrich, *Utopia in Power*, translated by Phyllis Carlos (New York: Summit Books, 1986), p. 190.

[23]Webb and Webb, p. 537, original emphasis.

[24]Boris Pasternak, quoted in Robert Conquest, *The Harvest of Sorrow* (New York: Oxford University Press, 1986), p. 10.

Also ignoring the evidence, British socialist John Strachey declared: "To travel from the capitalist world into Soviet territory is to pass from death to birth."[25] During the year in which Strachey penned these words, 4 million peasants were held in labor camps. No more than 10 percent were ever released and few survived beyond 1938.[26] Yet Strachey reported "an exhilaration of living which finds no parallel in the world."[27]

Intensified political commitments led others to excuse the terror. Novelist Upton Sinclair believed that social progress required the deaths of millions of people:

> They drove rich peasants off the land and sent them whole-sale to work in lumber camps and on railroads. Maybe it cost a million lives—maybe it cost 5 million—but you cannot think intelligently about it unless you ask yourself how many millions it might have cost if the changes had not been made.[28]

After a cursory look at the Soviet Union, American writers Corliss and Margaret Lamont claimed in 1933:

> All this is not to say that *already* in Russia certain aspects of living are not superior to those of the U.S. For instance, there is no unemployment there; the theory and practice of central planning have made great headway; legislation on behalf of workers is excellent; science is fast triumphing over superstition; the educational enthusiasm and achievements are very great; the attitude towards sex is frank and healthy; there has been a veritable liberation of women; race prejudice has all but disappeared; minority languages and cultures are being developed; and a true international spirit holds sway. Such things as these make up for many a temporary food shortage.[29]

[25]John Strachey, *The Coming Struggle for Power* (New York: Modern Library, 1935), p. 360. Originally published in 1933.

[26]Conquest, *The Harvest of Sorrow.*

[27]Strachey, p. 360.

[28]Upton Sinclair and Eugene Lyons, *Terror in Russia? Two Views* (New York: R. R. Smith, 1938), pp. 11–12.

[29]Corliss and Margaret Lamont, *Russia Day by Day: A Travel Diary* (New York: Covici, Friede, 1933), p. 257.

According to many writers, Stalin's purges of the Communist Party never occurred. Ingenuous observers believed that Stalin was indeed surrounded by hotbeds of rebellion, which he was well-justified in quelling. They accepted the far-fetched confessions of guilt from leaders of the Bolshevik Revolution without inquiring if they were extracted under torture. Several Western observers of the trials marveled at how the confessions agreed on tiny details, a factor that they cited as evidence of authenticity.

Joseph Davies, U.S. ambassador to the Soviet Union during 1936–38—the height of the purge trials—dismissed Stalin's destruction of his peers as follows: "To appraise the situation, it should be borne in mind that practically all of the principal defendants were bred from early youth in an atmosphere of conspiracy against established order. . . . Conspiracy was bred in the bone."[30] He considered the Soviet justice system to be exemplary: "The most extraordinary part of this trial, from a Western outlook, is that there should have been such a trial at all. The accused had all entered the plea of guilty."[31] Davies did not find it strange that high-ranking leaders in the Soviet government would be involved in a conspiracy to overthrow the government that they led. Rather, he thought the confessions showed that a "consistent vein of truth ran through the fabric, establishing a definite political conspiracy to overthrow the present government."[32] Davies bent over backwards to pay a further compliment to the Soviet justice system, finding in the show trials "a most powerful demonstration of the blessings that real constitutional protection of liberty affords."[33]

Victor Kravchenko, a former official in the Communist Party, provides a different perspective:

> I can attest that no one I met in Moscow attached the slightest value to their confessions. These men had consented to serve as puppets in a political morality play not in the least related to truth. Stalin was destroying his personal opponents and had succeeded in forcing them to participate in their own humiliation and extinction. We wondered about

[30]Joseph E. Davies, *Mission to Moscow* (New York: Simon and Schuster, 1941), p. 29.

[31]Ibid., p. 37.

[32]Ibid., p. 39.

[33]Ibid., p. 40.

the techniques he had used. But even Party people were not expected to believe the trial testimony literally. To do so would have been tantamount, among Communists, to an admission of congenital idiocy.[34]

Yet British historian Bernard Pares claimed: "Nearly all [defendants in the Bukharin trial] admitted having conspired against the life of Stalin and others, and on this point it is not necessary to doubt them."[35]

The Leninist doctrine of unconstrained power institutionalized evil in the Soviet system. Aleksandr Solzhenitsyn poignantly described some of the effects in his epic, The Gulag Archipelago 1918–1956, published in 1973, which told of a network of forced labor camps that stretched across the Soviet Union and devoured millions of lives. Solzhenitsyn revealed that Lenin put the system of slave labor in place. The camps, vastly enlarged by Stalin, became a mainstay of the Soviet economy.[36] Nobody was safe from sudden arrest and eventual induction into the ranks of forced laborers. Solzhenitsyn explained that the secret police "had over-all assignments, quotas for a specific number of arrests. These quotas might be filled on an orderly basis or wholly arbitrarily." He cited the instance of a woman who went to the Novocherkassk NKVD (secret police) to find out what to do with a baby orphaned by the arrest of a neighbor, only to end up tossed into a cell herself: "They had a total plan which had to be fulfilled in a hurry, and there was no one available to send out into the city—and here was this woman already in their hands!"[37]

Solzhenitsyn's account draws not only on his own personal sufferings but also on personal accounts of 227 other victims. The Communist Party's limitless power left the individual defenseless against the Soviet state. Millions were sentenced to the labor camps under broad interpretation of Article 58, Section 10, of the criminal

---

[34]Victor Kravchevko, I Chose Freedom (New Brunswick, N.J.: Transaction Publishers, 1989), p. 282. First published in 1946.

[35]Bernard Pares, A History of Russia (New York: Vintage Books, 1965), p. 542. First published in 1926.

[36]Aleksandr I. Solzhenitsyn, The Gulag Archipelago 1918-1956, abridged ed. (New York: Harper & Row, 1985), pp. 19–38. First published in 1973.

[37]Ibid., p. 9.

code: "Propaganda or agitation, containing an appeal for the over-throw, subverting, or weakening of the Soviet power . . . and, equally, the dissemination or preparation or possession of literary materials of similar content." Sentences of 10 or 25 years (equivalent to death sentences) were common for the punishment of invented infractions. Solzhenitsyn estimates that 60 million people lost their lives in the labor camps from 1918 to 1956.[38] Yet common criminals received sentences of six months to a year for robbery. The new Soviet state reasoned that criminal elements of Old Russia were just what the new regime needed to help bring about socialism. After all, they were assaulting private property. All they needed was re-education into the collective consciousness. The criminal was elevated to new heights. "Through its law the Stalinist power said to the thieves clearly: Do not steal from me! Steal from private persons! You see, private property is a belch from the past."[39] Robbery victims had little recourse. If they brought a case to court, the criminal received only a short sentence, oftentimes reduced for good behavior. Testifying against the offender often proved fatal for victims. Those criminals that did arrive at the labor camps were often used to terrorize political prisoners.

Barbaric conditions existed in the camps. Any camp keeper who was revolted by the evil and resisted degeneration into an inhuman monster soon became camp fodder himself.[40] Food rations were unlivable under any circumstances, and such meager food rapidly killed prisoners who were exhausted by 12-hour workdays in Sibe-rian subzero temperatures. Rations were calculated to squeeze the maximum work from a prisoner for about a year, while starving him to death to make way for the newly arriving hordes swept into the camps. Clothing supplies were nonexistent, and prisoners wore tattered rags to face the Arctic cold. People were reduced to a dying-animal existence. Solzhenitsyn describes death as sometimes taking the path of scurvy: "Your teeth begin to fall out, your gums rot, ulcers appear on your legs, your flesh will begin to fall off in whole chunks, and you will begin to smell like a corpse. Your bloated legs collapse." Other times it was pellagra: "Your face grows dark and

[38]Ibid., pp. xii, 19–38, 178.
[39]Ibid., p. 263.
[40]Ibid., p. 282.

your skin begins to peel and your entire organism is racked by diarrhea." Solzhenitsyn's portrait of a man dying of starvation smashed the rose-colored glasses that had kept reality away from the Western intellectual's assessment of Soviet life.[41]

It took Solzhenitsyn's skills to make the sufferings of the Gulag believable. Previous witnesses had lent their prestige to hoaxes set up by the Soviet government. The influential British intellectuals, Sidney and Beatrice Webb, denied the existence of forced labor camps: "The Soviet Government does not compel people to work, any more than the British and American Governments do."[42] They presented the Soviet penal system as a model of humane justice "which seems to go further, alike in promise and achievement, towards an ideal treatment of offenders against society than anything else in the world." The Webbs reported that prisoners are not locked up against their will but are "shown that a life of regulated industry and recreation, with the utmost practicable freedom, is more pleasant than a life of crime and beggary." The Webbs found such idyllic conditions that "many refuse to leave on the expiration of their sentences."[43]

A unique opportunity for exposure was squandered when Henry Wallace, vice president of the United States, visited the camps in 1944 and declared that the Soviets ran a model prison system. He visited Magadan, one of the largest and most notorious labor camps. Wallace failed to perceive any signs of forced labor at all, declaring, "I can bear witness to the willingness with which your citizens give their utmost efforts in mines, aircraft factories, and metallurgical works." Without perceiving the ghastly irony, he continued, "Men born in wide, free spaces will not brook injustice and tyranny. They will not even temporarily live in slavery."[44]

In 1977, Vladimir Bukovsky affirmed what Lenin himself had proudly stated—that there is no rule of law in the Soviet Union.[45] Bukovsky affirmed that even such protections for the individual as

[41]Ibid., pp. 227–28.

[42]Webb and Webb, p. 545.

[43]Webb and Webb, p. 484.

[44]Henry Wallace, *Soviet Asia Mission* (New York: Reynal and Hitchcock, 1946), pp. 136–37.

[45]Vladimir Bukovsky, *To Build a Castle—My Life as a Dissenter*, translated by Michael Scammell (New York: Viking Press, 1978).

exist in the Soviet Constitution are not observed. During the Stalin era, people were arrested arbitrarily while they went about their daily activities, such as shopping or going to work. Millions died, yet there were few real dissidents because people living in daily fear for their lives did not dare express any differences with the government. This fear affected the highest ranks of the Communist Party as well. To reassure the party, Khrushchev denounced Stalin in 1956 and broke the spell that had allowed people to accept a system of mendacity and lies. In Hungary in 1956 and in Czechoslovakia in 1968, party leaders announced that they had changed their minds and denounced the system they led. The political rebellions were crushed by Soviet tanks, but new ideas began to circulate and are now bearing fruit.

By the 1960s there really were dissidents in the Soviet Union. Moreover, the Soviet government was no longer willing to send large numbers of political prisoners to the Gulag. The government had progressed to the point where it was arresting *actual* dissidents, whether or not it could pin charges on them—a great improvement over the earlier Stalin regime.

Fearful for their own skins, the party leadership abandoned the Stalinist line of "the intensification of the class struggle" and replaced it with a new directive to the KGB known as the "intensification of psychiatric illnesses."[46] Real dissidents were classified as mentally ill and carted off to the psychiatric hospitals, and the party itself became safe.

The apologists of the 1930s and 1940s are often excused on the grounds that it was important to give the new socialist society the benefit of the doubt and that the facts were hard to ascertain. However, during the 1960s and 1970s and even the 1980s, many scholars were quick to find more success in the Soviet Union than was there. Just as the Webbs found in Stalinism a model constitution and Vice President Wallace saw a model penal system operating in the Gulag, in 1972 Professor Harold Berman of Harvard University found a rule of law in some modest penal reforms. He declared that "many of the basic concepts of Soviet criminal law and procedure are in the 'continental' tradition."[47] It is bizarre, to say the least, to

---

[46]Bukovsky, p. 196.

[47]Harold Berman, *Soviet Criminal Law and Procedure* (Cambridge: Harvard University Press, 1966), p. vi.

compare the Soviet penal system, which subjected political dissidents such as Bukovsky to torture in psychiatric hospitals, to the penal system of Western Europe. Similarly, in 1969 University of California professor Howard J. Sherman wrote that in the Soviet Union "managers are also in the unions and also receive their benefits, and this fact highlights the difference between Soviet and Western unions."[48] In 1984 economist John Kenneth Galbraith was still writing that "the Russian system succeeds because in contrast to the Western industrial economy it makes full use of its manpower."[49] By making comparisons such as these, scholars kept the true character of the Leninist state under wraps.

As it became more difficult to see the future in the Soviet model, hopes shifted to the Maoist model. In the early 1970s John Gurley, distinguished Stanford economist and former editor of the *American Economic Review*, saw the future in Maoist China. Artist Andy Warhol was sufficiently inspired by Maoism to create a romanticized larger-than-life mural of the dictator, which is still displayed in New York's Metropolitan Museum of Art.

By the end of the 1980s, the hopes were encamped in Marxist outposts in Latin America. Fidel Castro became a darling, and, until Daniel Ortega lost the elections in February 1990, leftists tried to discern a socialist utopia amidst Sandinista repression and the morass of the Nicaraguan economy. In July 1989 religious groups gathered in Washington to celebrate Ortega's rule. The Reverend Lucas Walker Jr., a member of Pastors for Peace, hailed the Sandinista tyranny, which deprived citizens of their rights and left Nicaragua the most impoverished country in the hemisphere, as "a dream that has inspired this whole hemisphere." Cecile Earle of Berkeley, California, insisted that under Ortega Nicaragua displayed "a different kind of poverty. There is poverty with dignity now, poverty with hope."[50]

Diehard apologists can still be found who deplore the reform process of the Soviet Union and cling to the old lies that have been discredited even in the Soviet Union. In March 1989, Alexander

[48]Howard Sherman, *The Soviet Economy* (Boston: Little, Brown, 1969), pp. 163–64.

[49]John Kenneth Galbraith, "Reflections: A Visit to Russia," *The New Yorker*, September 3, 1984, pp. 54–65.

[50]"The Sandinista Decade," editorial, *Washington Times*, July 20, 1989, p. F2

Cockburn, columnist for *The Nation*, dismissed Soviet historian Roy Medvedev's estimate that approximately 20 million died from forced labor, collectivization, famine, and the purges. "These heady days in Moscow," Cockburn wrote, "Soviet intellectuals will do anything to get their names in the papers."[51]

As late as 1988, Professor Jerry Hough of Duke University and the Brookings Institution continued to undercount the victims of the Great Purge[52] and insisted that no government-orchestrated famine in the Soviet Union ever occurred.

The economic reforms implemented by Gorbachev and Deng Xiaoping have run afoul of American journalists and professors who accuse these leaders of resurrecting greed. For example, *New York Times* journalist Bill Keller wrote that in the Soviet Union

> the sprouting of a new private sector has brought with it
> not only novel forms of corruption—among them extortion,
> money laundering, and conflicts of interest—but, it some-
> times seems, a general rise in the level of greed.[53]

The theme of pristine communist morality being soiled by private property is a favorite one of Arthur Schlesinger Jr., who complains that China's reforms brought an increase "in wealth, inequality and in corruption." He wonders when Deng Xiaoping will deal with the social costs—the rebirth of prostitution and greed—of letting the capitalist genie out of the bottle.[54]

The absolutism of the party's rule has spread corruption throughout every aspect of Soviet life. University students must bribe professors to get passing grades; parents must bribe teachers to stop them from victimizing their children in school; judges and police must be bribed to ensure favorable judgments, whether fair or unfair; doctors and nurses must be bribed for good and honest care; tribute must be paid to officials to gain respite from arbitrary power. Communism, which was to eliminate buying and selling,

---

[51]Alexander Cockburn, "Beat the Devil," *The Nation*, March 6, 1989, pp. 294–95.

[52]Jerry Hough, *Gorbachev and the Politics of Reform* (New York: Simon and Schuster, 1988), p. 69.

[53]Bill Keller, "Soviet Foray into Capitalism Begins to Show a Seamy Side," *New York Times*, July 25, 1988, p. A1.

[54]Arthur Schlesinger Jr., "At Last: Capitalistic Communism," *Wall Street Journal*, August 4, 1987, p. 34.

has succeeded in turning everything into a commodity—grades, scholarships, justice, decent treatment—nothing can be had without being purchased. Yet bribery and corruption should not come as a surprise. In a society where truth and justice have no independent standing and are defined in terms of the interest of the Communist Party, it is only natural that people put their trust in bribes.

Forced to participate in this system, the individual became chained to one side of himself—"the dark side"—unless he was willing to spend his life in prison or labor camps or the psychiatric ward. This all-inclusive, claustrophobic debauchment is unique to communist countries. Konstantin Simis observes that "the Soviet government, Soviet society, cannot rid itself of corruption as long as it remains Soviet,"[55] an assessment shared by Solzhenitsyn who says that communism is inimical to humanity and a denial of life itself.

Seventy years of Soviet communism has proved to be enough for the party's own leaders. Confronted with social and economic failure, Mikhail Gorbachev set about dismantling the Leninist state with his policy of glasnost, or openness. He permitted and encouraged Soviet citizens to speak their minds, and they did. People complained about economic failures and irrationality, privileges of the ruling class, unaccountable power, and unresponsive authorities. Intellectuals went after Stalin, Lenin, and the whole panoply of crimes.

On April 5, 1988, *Pravda* foreclosed on Western apologists:

> It is sometimes claimed that Stalin did not know about instances of lawlessness. He did not simply know about them, he organized them and directed them. Today this is a proven fact. The guilt of Stalin and his immediate entourage before the Party and the people for the mass repressions and lawlessness they committed is enormous and unforgivable.[56]

One month later, Vasily Selyunin assailed the Soviet Union's most revered icon: Lenin himself. He wrote in *Novy Mir* (May 1988),

[55]Konstantin Simis, *USSR: The Corrupt Society,* translated by Jacqueline Edwards and Mitchell Schneider (New York: Simon and Schuster, 1982), p. 300.

[56]"The Principles of Restructuring: The Revolutionary Nature of Thinking and Acting," editorial, *Pravda,* April 5, 1988, p. 2.

a popular journal among the elite, that Lenin made serious mistakes when he abolished private property and created a system of forced labor camps. Describing the period immediately following the 1917 Bolshevik Revolution, Selyunin asserted: "The repression spread without boundaries. At first, the repression was of the opponents of the revolution, then of potential opponents of the revolution and, finally, the repression became a means of economics." He said that Lenin laid the foundations for Joseph Stalin's forced-labor economy and massive repressions. The publication of Selyunin's article marked the first time that Lenin's policies were attacked in the Soviet press and signaled the end of the Leninist state.

Gorbachev believes that setting the party above the law destroyed the basis of a moral society. At the Communist Party Congress in June 1988, he called for the "creation of a socialist state based on the rule of law." The Central Committee approved his proposal, announcing that "State and party agencies, public organizations, labor collectives, and all officials and citizens should operate on a strictly legal basis."[57] Academician Abel Aganbegyan, a Gorbachev ally, wrote that throughout Soviet history "lawyers were people who had to make laws fit what had been decided" and complained that "we have no tradition of preparing formal, especially legal, documents." Aganbegyan praised the June 1988 Party Conference for formulating "a plan to turn the Soviet State into a legal state in which the law would indeed be supreme."[58]

February 7, 1990, marked a turning point in world history. On that day the Communist Party repudiated Article 6 of the Soviet Constitution and stripped itself of its monopoly on power. The same party conference endorsed the principle of private property. As stated in the party platform, "the C.P.S.U. believes the existence of individual property, including ownership of the means of production, does not contradict the modern stage in the country's economic development."

This shift signifies the end of the totalitarian state. Communism, said Soviet foreign minister Eduard Shevardnadze, "has been destroyed by the will of peoples who wished no longer to tolerate

[57]The CPSU Central Committee's Theses for the 19th All-Union Party Conference, *Pravda*, May 27, 1988, pp. 1–3, and *Izvestiya*, May 27, 1988, pp. 1–2.

[58]Abel Aganbegyan, *Inside Perestroika: The Future of the Soviet Economy*, translated by Helen Szamuely (New York: Harper & Row, 1989), pp. 107, 203.

142

coercion."[59] The communists learned that Leninism dissolved the natural conduits of society and made life irrational and inhumane. Voluntary society is reemerging in the Soviet Union. Under Gorbachev's encouragement, independent organizations are springing up; religion is encouraged; traditional morality is sanctioned; art, literature, and the media are regaining their independence; and Marxism is even being edited out of school textbooks. Another dictator could arise, but he would be a mere authoritarian, restrained by law and voluntary associations.

The dream of Marxist utopia, which caused the deaths of millions in the 20th century, has been expelled from the Soviet Union. Its last refuge is in American church groups and academic faculties. Abandoned by a Soviet regime that is embracing the economic institutions and human values of Western civilization, our alienated intellectuals have no Marxist societies left to defend. It remains to be seen whether they will rediscover the virtues of a free society or become more fanatical in their attack on Western civilization.

Intellectuals, proclaiming their social conscience, have inflicted untold destruction on humanity in the 20th century. They demanded that the sphere of private property and economic liberty be ever more tightly circumscribed. However, today the old Marxist model of the worker exploited by the capitalist has lost all meaning as increasingly the state prevents everyone—both worker and capitalist—from realizing his or her potential. In an interview with Sotsialisticheskaya Industriya, Soviet economist Yaroslav Kuzminov said:

> No normal capitalist, with the exception of a very narrow stratus of rentiers, who have now been reduced to a minimum in the countries of the West, can boast that he does not work. He very often works with greater effort and more efficiently than his employees. . . . How does this capitalist develop at the expense of workers? It is not by chance that the concept of exploitation had practically disappeared from economic thinking in the West by the second half of the 20th century.[60]

[59]TASS, February 5, 1990, cited in "Notable & Quotable," Wall Street Journal, February 28, 1990.

[60]Ye. Leontyeva, "We Discuss the Draft Law on Ownership: To Strengthen Stability Against Misfortune?" Moscow Sotsialisticheskaya Industriya, December 12, 1989, p. 2.

As the 20th century comes to a close, people all over the world have come to understand that exploitation results from the imposition of coercive restrictions by the state. Whether in China, the Soviet Union, socialist Europe, statist America, or the government-devastated economies of the Third World, no one outside the ruling nomenklaturas any longer views government as the instrument of social progress. The commitment of Western academics and World Bank officials to industrial policy and development planning has outlived the commitment of the Chinese student and worker, the Soviet economist, and the Third World peasant. The reemergence of private property and economic freedom out of communism is the greatest victory that liberal society has ever achieved. Naysayers in Western intellectual ranks, such as Arthur Schlesinger Jr., who warn that private property will mean the reappearance of greed and prostitution, demonstrate by their doubts their lack of commitment to a free society.

Whatever else it does, the demise of Marxism-Leninism will cause a renaissance in Western scholarship. For decades we have explained ourselves in terms of power, profit, and economic interests. Marx's view—that the character of individuals and the nature of society are determined by economic interests—permeates the study of history and society and has made almost every Western achievement and institution seem illegitimate. Moreover, to the extent that we have been influenced by them, the Marxian explanations have worsened our character as a people, because, as the old saying goes, "a person becomes what he thinks he is."

Never before has the world seen such a privileged and powerful organization as the Communist Party of the Soviet Union. If material interests are the determining force in history, why is the Communist Party giving up its own? Its consent to its own demise proves that good will can prevail over material interest; and this will revive idealistic explanations dismissed by Marx as fantasy. As our explanations of our free society become less denunciatory and more positive, the West will become a better example for those countries struggling to regain a humane existence.

Index

145

147

148

economic planning concept of, 76–77
materialist interpretation of history, 75
Marxism
  alienation and violence concepts in, 127
  effect of demise of, 144
  effect of myths of economic history, 122–23
Marxism-Leninism-Stalinism, 126–27
Marxist organizations, Russia, 77–78
Materialist concept of history, 75–76, 77, 144
Medical care system. *See also* Disease; Health problems; Mortality rates; Rural areas
  hierarchal nature of, 56
  hospitals and clinics in, 57–62
  ranking of facilities in, 62
  in rural areas, 65
Memorial, 99
Mensheviks, 77
Mironov, B., 55n, 56n, 60, 61n, 64n
Molchanov, V., 12
Moral standards, 97–98, 140
  denial in communism of, 126–27, 129
  emphasis on revival of, 95–98
  in Western philosophy, 124–26
Morgun, F. T., 34–35
Mortality rates, 36, 62, 117, 122, 132
Morton, Henry, 52n
Moscow, 91
Moscow Province, 51
Moscow River, 35
Murzin, A., 65n

Nasar, Rusi, 33n
Nationalism, Russian, 118–19
Nationalization, 78, 125
Nekrich, Aleksandr, 132
Net output indicator, 8
New Economic Policy (1921), 79–80. *See also* Commodity production
Niazov, Grigory, 98
Nicaragua, 139
Nikitin, A., 21n
Noginsk, 51
Nomenklatura. See Bureaucratic class (*nomenklatura*)

Ortega, Daniel, 139

Oryol, A., 20n

Pakov Province, 65
Palmer. R. R., 122n
Pares, Bernard, 135
Pasternak, Boris, 132
Penal system. *See* Labor camps
Perestroika
  effect of, 43, 93, 109–10
  as retreat from central planning, 79
  signals of success for, 106
  Soviet citizen perception of, 41–43
Petrograd, 78
Pharmaceutical industry, 58
Pinsker, Boris, 109
Piyesheva, Larisa, 109
Plans. *See* Factory plan
Pokrovskiy, Vadim, 63
Polanyi, Michael, 124–25, 129–30
Politburo, 131
Political influences in factories, 26–29
Political reform, 92–95, 98–100, 117. *See also* Election reform
  during economic reform transition, 116
Pollution. *See also* Health problems; Mortality rates
  of air, 32–33, 35
  from heavy metals, 61
  prohibition of individual monitoring for, 35
  of water, 33–34, 36, 60
Prager, Kenneth, 59
Premiums. *See* Bonuses and premiums
Price system. *See also* Black market; Shortages
  abolition under Stalin of, 81–82
  freedom to adjust for, 116
  reform of, 103–5
  without relationship to market value, 14
Private enterprise system, 25–26, 67, 84–85
  See also Black market; Supply system
Private sector, 96
Privatization, 114–16, 117
Production input
  competition for, 84–85
  destruction of value of, 32
  effect of factory self-sufficiency for, 15–16
Production output
  effect of gross output system on, 10–14

About the Authors

Paul Craig Roberts holds the William E. Simon Chair in Political Economy at the Center for Strategic and International Studies and is chairman of the Institute for Political Economy, a senior research fellow at the Hoover Institution, and an adjunct scholar at the Cato Institute. He is a former assistant secretary of the Treasury for economic policy and a former associate editor of, and columnist for, the *Wall Street Journal.* He is currently a columnist for *Business Week,* the Scripps Howard News Service, and the *Washington Times.* In 1987 he was awarded the Legion of Honor, France's highest award. Roberts is a member of the board of directors of Value Line Investment Funds, a member of the international advisory board of Wright Investors' Service, a member of the board of Marvin & Palmer, and an adviser to Morgan Guaranty Trust Company, Lazard Freres Asset Management, and other money managers. He is the author of three books, *The Supply-Side Revolution, Alienation and the Soviet Economy,* and *Marx's Theory of Exchange, Alienation, and Crisis,* and numerous articles in scholarly journals.

Karen LaFollette is a research associate at the Institute for Political Economy in Washington, D.C. She is currently researching a book on the failure of development planning in Latin America.

Cato Institute

Founded in 1977, the Cato Institute is a public policy research foundation dedicated to broadening the parameters of policy debate to allow consideration of more options that are consistent with the traditional American principles of limited government, individual liberty, and peace. Toward that goal, the Institute strives to achieve a greater involvement of the intelligent, concerned lay public in questions of policy and the proper role of government.

The Institute is named for *Cato's Letters*, pamphlets that were widely read in the American Colonies in the early 18th century and played a major role in laying the philosophical foundation for the revolution that followed. Since that revolution, civil and economic liberties have been eroded as the number and complexity of social problems have grown.

To counter this trend the Cato Institute undertakes an extensive publications program dealing with the complete spectrum of policy issues. Books, monographs, and shorter studies are commissioned to examine the federal budget, Social Security, regulation, NATO, international trade, and a myriad of other issues. Major policy conferences are held throughout the year, from which papers are published thrice yearly in the *Cato Journal*.

In order to maintain an independent posture, the Cato Institute accepts no government funding. Contributions are received from foundations, corporations, and individuals, and other revenue is generated from the sale of publications. The Institute is a nonprofit, tax-exempt, educational foundation under Section 501(c)3 of the Internal Revenue Code.

CATO INSTITUTE
224 Second St., S.E.
Washington, D.C. 20003